A PORTRAIT OF THE HOLY SPIRIT

Paul Larson

A Portrait of the Holy Spirit
by Paul Larson

Printed in the United States of America

ISBN 9781612158297

www.xulonpress.com

CONTENTS

INTRODUCTION

God is Spirit. The Holy Spirit is God. A spirit is not visible. How then can I paint a portrait of the Holy Spirit? The answer is that although I have been painting pictures in oil for over forty years I cannot paint a portrait in the usual way. I can, however, produce a likeness in an unusual way. I can produce a "word" picture. The picture on the cover is an oil painting which I produced of my wife and I from a photo taken by our daughter Naomi at her daughter's wedding dance in Birmingham, Alabama, on New Years Eve 2010. It portrays an image of ourselves but does not examine why, when or who we really are.

The Portrait of the Holy Spirit I seek to paint in the text you are about to read has a narrative of many unusual and sometimes disjointed events in my life, in the events of my family, of my friends, of churches, and finally a wave that many persons lived through in the 1960s, '70s, '80s, and beyond. If you view the narrative as merely a biography or one of interesting events you are viewing the narrative from the wrong perspective. You should view them as though you are putting oil on a canvass and each event or story as a single brush stroke which taken together forms a portrait of the Holy Spirit. Keep in mind that the author of the Bible is the Holy Spirit. Not a single photo was used but it remains the greatest story ever told!

Strengthen the feeble hands
Steady the knees that give Way;
Say to those with feeble hearts
'Be strong, do not fear;
Your god will come,
He will come with vengeance,
With divine retribution
He will come to save you.
Then will the eyes of the blind
Be opened
And the ears of the deaf unstopped.
Then will the lame leap like
Deer,...
Is. 35; 3-5

Chapter One

THE MAKING OF A LAME MAN
(Where is God?)

T he winters in North Dakota in mid-January are long, cold and dark. The darkness was especially apparent as I lay on my back and stared upward at the stars. The deep darkness of the night caused each star to have the appearance of miniature suns that danced and twinkled in an entertaining display.

As I continued to lay there a gathering awareness of the situation moved into the reality of my mind. The reality was cold. It was accompanied by the awareness of something uncomfortable and hard beneath my head. Soon a commotion caused me to look around and see that there were many persons who had gathered around me in a circle and each seemed to be gesturing and pointing at me but saying little. Soon they moved to make way for my sister Dorothy who had emerged from within the towing car. She confronted me and said "Get up Paul! " I replied that I had tried to get up but I could not and there was something hurting me under my head! Again she said "Get up!" Then she and others reached out and pulled me up. They were met by my screams as the "hard feeling" behind my head fell to the ground. It was my foot still in its overshoe. It dangled from the broken bone above the knee and it was impossible to stand.

The stillness of the night was now broken with shouts and explanations that the toboggan pulled behind my cousin's car had been run over by an approaching vehicle. The driver had been unable to see an eleven year old boy in his headlights until the thud of impact made him painfully aware. It also startled me to realize that I was that boy and I was seriously injured.

The pain overwhelmed me as several boys lifted me on to the toboggan and began to pull me by hand to the house of my Uncle Karl. The pain was multiplied because my leg repeatedly fell off the side of the toboggan. The broken bones ground together as I was hauled along. I continually shouted at those pulling the toboggan that my leg was floating away and they should pull it down. Eventually the somber group surrounding the toboggan arrived at the house where the older folks including my mother and dad talked excitedly about what could be done.

World War II had reached its zenith in January of 1945 and would soon sputter to an end in Europe. Unfortunately it was too late to avoid a family tragedy which had occurred some weeks earlier. The son of Karl and his wife Emma was an excellent student but because of the distance of their farm from a high school they arranged to have Willard live in our family for three years much of the time until he received his diploma. He had become a virtual big brother. The following year after his high school graduation he attended Concordia College in Moorhead Minnesota where he was a pre-med student. He was drafted for the army early in 1944, and received his basic training, became a corporal and was immediately sent to France as a replacement where he was killed. The Hannaford community laid him to rest in the local cemetery in October. Very sad. All those events within a year but those were sad times. Now I was the cause of multiplied anxiety to those family and friends gathered in the cold not knowing how they could help.

Two doctors served the entire county of Griggs. They were over worked, elderly and unavailable when called. A nurse who served one of the doctors agreed to come quickly and within the hour drove twelve miles from her county seat home in Cooperstown. She splinted my injured leg with gauze over a LOOK magazine and placed me on the living room couch.

My mother sat with me as I fought the pain and the shock of the injury. Throughout the long night I laid awake and listened to the sound of the loud ticking of a clock. By morning nothing had changed but the older folks had now determined that I must be moved to St. Luke's hospital in Fargo, North Dakota where I could receive the care of an orthopedic doctor. Uncle Karl agreed to drive his car which was newer and more comfortable. Mother and Dad joined him to comfort me and make hospital arrangements.

Arrangements for the trip itself moved slowly. Another day elapsed before the journey began. Late in the evening of the second day I was admitted to the hospital and because of the great crowding due to the war I was placed on the fourth cot in the furnace room. Late that night the harried doctor was ushered to my bedside to determine what he could do for me. An X-ray taken the previous afternoon revealed a crushed femur bone about four inches above the knee. There was no evidence of more broken bones but my body was badly bruised.

Dr. Swanson, the orthopedic surgeon, carefully removed the LOOK magazine and felt my injured leg with his hands. I would feel those hands many times in the months that followed. The hands were easy to distinguish. I later learned that prior to his becoming a surgeon he had been a butcher and had lost most of his fingers at the second joint in a meat saw accident. Shortly after our meeting he visited with my parents and informed them that my leg should be amputated! They prevailed on him to try to save the leg and he agreed to try. The next morning he began surgery.

A combination of ether and gas kept me asleep for hours. When I awoke I was violently ill. The ether smell lingered and I vomited for what seemed like hours. Gradually I returned to life and learned that an incision about eight inches long on the side of the leg had been made to expose the bone. Dr. Swanson cleaned out the bone chips and placed a metal plate on the bone. The plate was fastened to the bone with four screws about one inch long. He then closed the wound by stitching it shut and declared it a successful operation. A full length cast held the leg rigid from hip to toe.

Three days later I became aware that all was not completely well with the surgery. My temperature was rising and the incision was pulling apart in the stitches. Soon the wound began to drain and the doctor ordered "sulfa" drugs, the major advance in fighting infection. Later I learned that it was quite common to contract staff infection when having surgery in any hospital at that time, I also began to realize that what I thought was ending was only beginning. The fight was now not merely to save my leg but to save my life.

The use of sulfa drugs was completely useless in my situation as the incision broke open. Dr. Swanson ordered the nurses to prepare me for another surgery to close the wound. Again after the surgery I was violently ill from the ether and my temperature refused to return to normal.

A child on the edge of death seemed to energize the entire hospital staff and a new plan emerged. It required the use of a new drug previously used exclusively among the wounded military and termed penicillin. It was hurriedly transported by air to Fargo from Minneapolis. The drug looked like maple syrup and was retained in a cold condition. It was also very painful when inserted into my tiny buttocks. The fight began with a new shot every three or four hours and went around the clock for a total of 64 shots. I dreaded the shots and counted each one. Finally after two weeks my temperature returned to normal. I had won another temporary victory.

The time went very slowly throughout the physical struggle. My thoughts often turned to "why am I here?" Surely God was behind these events. My knowledge of God was elementary but a statue in the front of our Lutheran church portrayed Jesus as a loving God carefully carrying a lamb in his protective arms. I felt like the lamb but without his protection.

Where was he? How could he ignore me so? I was angry that he could not find me and I wondered about life's value for me. Perhaps it would be best to just give up and die!

My return home to family lifted my thoughts and life returned to a more normal routine with monthly visits to Fargo to have an X-ray and occasionally have the full length cast replaced. The partly healed incision required Dad to paint the wound with "silver nitrate" daily as it continued to drain. He was up to the task and we made an event of each dressing change. Gradually the wound healed.

A hospital bed had been placed in the living room next to the radio when I first returned home. It was while I lay there that I heard the disturbing news that the only President of the United States that I had heard of had died. I wondered if the nation could continue on without President Roosevelt.

The news of his passing was soon followed by the news that Germany had surrendered and the war in Europe was over. There was great celebrating with the ringing of church bells and happy celebrations but the news was dimmed by the realization that the war remained to be fought in Japan.

The X-rays continued to show that the shattered bone was healing and forming a protective shield like an automobile tire around the bone. I was told that when the healing was complete the injured leg would be stronger than the uninjured leg. Unfortunately other problems continued to appear.

When the full length cast was removed the knee held unbent by the cast refused to bend. Atrophy was the term used to describe the condition in which a knee not continuously bent became as rigid as the bone. The atrophy became most apparent when the full length cast was replaced by a half-length cast from my hip to the knee. Dr. Swanson predicted that exercise with time would return the knee to normal. In the meantime I hobbled with a single crutch aiding the injured leg.

With the school year beginning in the fall of 1945 I was determined to be a normal fifth grader. At recess time one day a pick up football game developed and I said I would play back and knock down passes! A classmate ran into our defending backfield with his head down and unseeing he knocked me down. I fell and tried to break my fall with my injured leg. The knee refused to bend and I felt pain above my knee. I thought it would soon pass. It did not but I was due for my trip to Fargo for X-rays and doctor visit so I ignored the discomfort. Dr. Swanson was visibly concerned when I met my appointment and he told me the news that my knee which refused to bend when I fell had broken the bone above the knee with a "green stick fracture" and was healing in a bent position. Without explaining about what he was about to do he asked my Dad and another man to hold me with my leg extended out straight from where I was seated in a wheel chair. The doctor took a position above my leg and quickly forced my leg down with a chop of his hand without anesthetic to break the healing green stick fractured bone back into a normal position. He next replaced the full length cast and sent me home. Time passed and the "greenstick fracture" healed along with the original fracture. Although it sounds cruel it was probably no more cruel then adding one more surgery to the already total of five with its accompanying ether aftermath.

At the next doctor visit the world I was getting used to be shattered once more when Dr. Swanson explained to me that the greenstick fracture had injured the growth center in the femur bone. I learned that a bone grows from each end and the end above the knee would not continue to grow when I matured into adulthood. He explained that the uninjured leg would have to have the similar growth center stopped or I would have one leg shorter than the other and I would be permanently lame. Again I thought of another surgery with its ether and pain. I sobbed and said I could not stand another operation. Dr. Swanson looked at me and began to cry as well. Then he hugged me tight, sent me home and did not mention further surgery again.

After months of waiting the last cast was cut off. The leg had shrunk dramatically and was cold to the touch. The knee had a bend of perhaps four inches and walking was labored. Dr. Swanson recommended riding a bike and walking. Gradually the knee moved in a larger arc. My new goal was to be able to sit on a chair and have my foot hang straight down to the floor. Each little pressure on the knee was painful but eventually I was able to ride a bike if the seat was raised up high.

One day while Dad and I were walking down the main street of Valley City. North Dakota in front of store windows I looked to see my reflection and noticed that I was limping. Dad became aware that I was observing my walk so he stopped also and asked me in a stern voice "can't you walk without limping?" I felt hurt because he rarely spoke to me in an accusing voice. In addition I had not realized how short my injured leg had become and how pronounced the limp. The prophecy that Dr. Swansen earlier pronounced had come to pass. Now what could I do? Perhaps I could improve. From that time on I practiced whenever I could see my image. I learned that both legs had to be the same length of stride and to accomplish that I had to bend my uninjured leg when I strode with that leg. I became so good at the shuffle that developed that unless I had to walk fast or run few people knew that I was lame. It never occurred to me at that time to ask God for help!

A FAMILY PHOTO -If a photo was available from the time of the mid 1930s one would see Halvor Johnson, a Norwegian immigrant to America who had developed a productive North Dakota farm located ten miles south east of Hannaford. He would be sitting in a rocking chair in the living room of the home that he had constructed in Hannaford. He is a tall elderly man with a cropped white beard wearing a dark cardigan sweater and dark trousers. His shoes are high to the ankle typical of the elderly. Beside him on the floor is a large red can of pipe tobacco, the fuel for his pipe which he frequently smoked. Not pictured is Anna, a stout Norwegian woman Halvor met and married on a visit to his home in Norway but who had recently passed away. Together they were Norwegian Lutheran Christians. They were strong in their faith and pillars in the Hannaford Lutheran church.

The very tall three hundred pound man standing to his right is Karl, their first born. He now "ran the farm." He would inherit the farm and the house in town. The two athletic young men standing to his left are Albert and Joe, (each well-educated lawyers) and the tall, slim attractive woman to the right of the young men was their daughter Ellen (my mother). Two persons not pictured were Henry the strong healthy second son who died in the influenza epedemic of 1919. The other girl named Hazel was born an epileptic and died at the age of fourteen during a grand mall seizure.

Chapter Two

BORN AGAIN
(Convicted of the Need of Jesus as Savior)

A Saturday afternoon three years after my leg injury our FARGO FORUM newspaper was at the post office waiting to be carried home. I had walked to the post office from our home in Hannaford. North Dakota. The return walk began with the paper in my hand. The post office was a large concrete block building located at the North end of Main Street. I walked out of the building and stood on the curb of a gravel road. Much of the road approaching from the South crossed an overhead that allowed the East/West travel of Great Northern railroad trains. (A branch line of the Northern Pacific paralleled the main street through town.)

My walk crossed Main Street past the lumber yard, over the N.P. tracks and stopped briefly at the large mercantile building. I paused there several minutes while I watched people buying groceries and other needs. Then I continued west past the telephone office, Bill Weller's machine shop and paused again before a falling down livery barn. Here a memory of three or four boys who used to stand by the door and who tried to frighten young children including myself as we walked by the barn intruded on my mind. I also recalled a story that my "big brother" Willard had fought with them and chased them away. With that happy thought I walked on. The sidewalk continued west with box elder trees lining the area between the sidewalk and the road. There at the corner of the block was Palmer Flesjer's house who was our neighbor and across the street to the south was the imposing two story white house which my Grandfather Halvor Johnson built in the 1920s. It was the house my Uncle Karl now occupied and the house I had been carried into on the toboggan.

On the corner to the west across the street from Uncle Karl's house was the stucco walled Presbyterian Church. North of that church on the fourth of the corner lots was the large white Norwegian Lutheran Church. It was a typical frontier church with a large bell tower. The bell when it rang to call people to church or tolled for the passing of a parishioner had a sound easily distinguished from that of the Presbyterian Church across the street.

Our two story house was located directly North behind the Lutheran Church. Our house was a part of my mother's inheritance. Her Father had a large sum of money in a local bank when it declared bankruptcy in the early 1920s. In the settlement that followed he received eight houses in Hannaford. Ours was one of those houses.

As I stood facing our Lutheran Church I was uneasy because I knew I had a very important decision to make. In the morning I would be among several persons of my age to be "confirmed." As a child I had been water baptized by Pastor Lee. That had required my parent's decision. Now I had to confirm that decision. I had to answer the question in a service "Do you want to accept Jesus as your personal savior?—Yes or No."

The answer "no" was unthinkable. It was my parents wish to hear "yes" from me. It was my wish as well. But... my mind returned to the dreadful days in the hospital when I asked God "how could you let this happen to me?" I forced the negative thought from my mind and resolved that my answer in the service would be "yes." With that problem settled I walked the rest of the way home.

A FAMILY PHOTO— If a photo was available from the mid-1930s one would see a woman named Mina Larson in her seventies. She is dressed in a brown dress and shoes similar to other elderly ladies of the day. Her hair is gathered in a knot behind her head. Her hair is gray, not white. Beside her is her daughter Mary Larson. She is tall and slim but quite muscular for a woman. She has never married and her career is taking care of her mother Mina and a young boy named Robert (Dan's son not pictured) Next to Mina is her eldest son Daniel. Beside him is his younger brother Louis (my father) Dan and Louis have shared a custom farming operation and a small manufacturing business. Not pictured is Annie a daughter who married young and moved to Canada. Also Andrew, Mina's husband who had recently died.

A SNAPSHOT - (an actual photo in an obscure box somewhere dated 1956) the picture is of a young man dressed in a college graduation gown. He holds a golf club in a position ready to drive the ball. The club is a gift from his parents marking graduation from Concordia College in Moorhead Minnesota.

(Author comment) I had graduated from High School in Hannaford in 1952.

Our school was deficient in science and math like many North Dakota schools at that time The school did excel in business education and reading courses (and of course, basketball) My choice of colleges was the University of North

Dakota which I had briefly visited for a music competition. Despite my choice when it was time to attend college there was strong reasons for choosing Concordia. Although the school was best known for music and its concert choir it also emphasized religion courses. My sister Dorothy majored in music there but my interest in music was pure country. Several reasons accounted for my attendance at Concordia. Mother attended the Academy there. Dorothy graduated from there and would soon marry the college registrar. My brother Donnie spent a year there, cousin Robert and most of my Johnson cousins as well. My leg injury prevented college level basketball competition and my parents would support me in return for summer work on the farm. That was an offer I could not refuse. Four years of classes with majors in history and political science, daily chapel exercises and many religious courses resulted in a B.A. degree and a three year tuition scholarship to Valaparaiso University Law School in Indiana. I had coveted an opportunity to attend law school since I was in the fifth grade.

A SNAPSHOT -A large building named Eidfjord Luthwran Church loomed large in the background and on the steps a number of young boys and girls who attended a vacation Bible school posed for a photo. On the end was my sister Dorothy who as a college student served as the teacher. In the middle was a tall pig tailed girl who seemed to be a leader of the group. Her name was Betty Michaelson and her parent's farm was located only a few hundred yards to the west.

A STUDIO PHOTO: The Omer Michelson family. Seated in front is Omer identified by his "farmer tan." Seated beside him is his wife Myrtle. Standing in the back are Jim and Gordon, already adult men. In the middle of the row is Betty and beside her are her two teen age brothers Merle and Harlyn (Bud.) They are wearing their best clothes and together are ready to reveal their lives in the early 1950s.

Chapter 3

CHANGE OF COURSE
(The Holy Spirit as Counselor)

The day was cloudy in Valparaiso Indiana. I drove my Pontiac car to the law building that day as usual because the law building was separate from the under graduate campus where I lived. Several weeks had passed since I set out driving from our farm at Hannaford. I drove alone and with a noticeable anxiety as I had never traveled very far into Minnesota or any states to the East. The road was four lane, comfortable driving and uneventful. When I viewed Minneapolis my thought was "Wow" it was so big. Several hours of driving later I first viewed Chicago. My thought was "Wow, wow, wow" at its giant size. Forty five miles farther south and I reached Valparaiso. At the University I was assigned a room in a barracks building apparently obtained from an army camp no longer in use. I was assigned a "cell" perhaps eight feet wide and ten feet long with a single bunk and a desk. Not what I had imagined! After the first shock of the place wore off I had settled down to the realization that I was alone, in a strange place and not very happy. It seemed the future would have to improve.

One day as I approached the law building I realized that something was different. A small café adjacent to the law building was completely destroyed. The windows were gone, the walls were full of holes and the inside was completely gutted. I parked my car and entered the law building where I asked the secretary what had happened to the "Green Door." the name of the café that had been destroyed. She replied that apparently the café management had been using the wrong brand of pizza. Wrong in the eyes of the Chicago "mob" and a gang of men had appeared at night. They had sprayed the building with machine gun fire that completely destroyed the building. I knew then that I was a long way from the farm at Hannaford.

The weeks passed and my law studies continued. My average day involved two or three hours of listening to lectures on subjects such as contracts, agency, torts, procedure, and property. There were usually no tests during the term. Instead there was "case briefings" That involved reading the opinion of a judge on a case and condensing the opinion in a "brief book." The question of the law needed to be determined and a conclusion stated. On the desk top in my barracks a Black's law dictionary laid permanently open. It allowed legal words and phrases to be interpreted when reading an opinion. My average day of briefing involved three or four different case briefings each day and usually every day. Although it was hard work it would not have seemed difficult if it had been in the subject of history.

Soon I began asking the question of myself "what ever happened to living?" Why am I in this unhappy position? Only an occasional case interested me. Eventually I concluded the reason went back to my youth and it involved two of my lawyer uncles. Albert who had a thriving law practice and Joe who was one of the original G-men under J. Edger Hoover and who retired as the bureau chief in Denver. Both Joe and Albert spent several fall days each year in the

Hannaford area where we would all hunt pheasants and ducks. I realized after much thought that I was influenced by my uncles not by their law careers which I knew nothing about.

I also realized that the most successful students in my classes were usually older or experienced people such as businessmen or returning army veterans. Often they had lived many similar situations described in the cases and could see both sides to legal questions more easily. I was young, inexperienced and from an "ivory tower" life. When tests came and they did usually at the end of a year or a semester I was only average. Previously when I entered a classroom as an under graduate student I always knew that in history or other reading subjects such as religion, that I would be in a small group at the top of the class.

These conflicts coupled with lonely hard work allowed me only one sub-conscious escape mechanism, I began having a nervous affliction termed "colitis" an uncomfortable bowel problem which if left alone is serious. One night I awoke from sleep and began to ponder the various life problems which beset me. Then not expecting it an overwhelming anxiety came over me. I arose and paced the hallway and tried to relax but it worsened I didn't know where to turn. I may have prayed a bit but it was not my first idea to turn to God for answers. I later learned that I was enduring a somewhat common experience termed a "panic attack." To me it was as serious as the experience on the toboggan and its aftermath. The night ended and I regrouped but I knew one thing for sure. I could not live like that and something would have to change. I probably had to end my law school days temporarily or permanently at the end of the term. I returned to the farm still unclear of the future.

During the summer my brother in law told me that he knew a Christian counselor who might be able to tell me why I was suffering from anxiety and related discomforts.

At that time anyone that visited a counselor risked being labeled a crazy guy. Mental hospitals were termed insane asylums and the treatments were more dangerous than the illness. Nevertheless I overcame my fears and contacted him. Fortunately I found him to be on the leading edge of his profession. He began by administering a battery of tests and then carefully explaining the results. Happily I was not psychotic. Translation: I was not crazy. He followed that announcement by teaching me what the literature knew about my discomfort. He greatly reduced my anxiety with information. He pointed to my serious injury at a formative time in my life as a contributing factor. He also suggested that I had been overprotected leading to fears of many things I could not control. Thus anxiety! My future comfort required careful planning and wise decisions throughout my life. A sign on his wall proclaimed in large letters 'LET GO AND LET GOD' He highly recommended that advice. It sounded like good advice but it would require living and learning.

In mid-summer while I worked on the farm I had applied for any kind of work available through the placement service at Concordia College. Then when the harvest was partially complete I received a phone call. The call was from a superintendent of schools at a little town in west central Minnesota which I never knew existed named Tintah. He opened the conversation with the words "my coach has quit. Come down and help me out until I can hire a replacement." I was surprised and a bit amused. He further explained that his coach was a crop spray pilot and the season conflicted with school teaching and he chose the spraying. I replied by telling him that I did not have a teaching certificate. Indeed I did have a minor in education but because of the law school scholarship I had not completed student teaching. Oh, he said "that was no problem. Just come right away and he would take care of that." Then as a parting incentive he added "the pheasant hunting is great here." With that parting statement he changed my reluctance into a passionate acceptance of his invitation. The next day I met a young ambitious school superintendent, visited several classrooms and was scheduled to teach the next day. As I prepared for bed that night I pondered the previous two days activities and I wondered is this the "let God" part of the sign in the counselors office beginning to go into action?

My recent past was preparing for law school classes. The next day I would be teaching classes of students from the seventh to the twelfth grades. The material I prepared for the next day would last for weeks. The kids were patient with my lack of experience and I finished the day tired but happy. The happy feeling continued throughout the week and then the month. Superintendent Mjolsness was delighted as well and together we laid plans to obtain my teaching certificate. An education instructor from Concordia agreed to work with the superintendent and within a few weeks I was a genuine certified teacher. The older experienced teachers aided me with the problems that always inevitably arise. My most comforting comment came from the principal at the end of each day when she entered the teacher's coffee room with the observation that in a hundred years who will know the difference? I was learning that I could cope with the stresses of teaching. Besides I did not have time with teaching, coaching and preparation for each day to consider failure. I loved my work and besides I had earned $3,950.00 for the first years' work.

When my third year of teaching at Tintah ended Supt. Mjolsness resigned his position, moved on to a new position, called me to join the same staff with him at Lake Park and I readily agreed. I was now a successful teacher looking to improve my career. I was already seeking to improve my history abilities by beginning a masters program at the University of North Dakota which I could pursue during the summer vacation months.

Chapter 4

THE LOVE CHAPTER

S unday was a beautiful sunshiny spring day in Lake Park. The baseball season was always short in Minnesota in the spring and I knew from experience that every good day no matter when in the week had to be used some way to improve the baseball skills of the players. I spread the word among the players to come to the playing field for an afternoon of practice. The practice went well. They returned to the dressing room which I had opened for them. When everyone was gone I locked the building and prepared to leave when Swede Michaelson ran toward me and said "I forgot my billfold in the dressing room and it had money in it. Would you let me back into the building to get it? "He also said that his aunt Betty was waiting for him in her car. I opened the door and thought to myself "I know her so I wandered over to her car to talk about events from back home. The memory I had of her was as a pre-teen with pig tails when my sister Dorothy had taught vacation Bible school at the Eidfjord Lutheran Church near her family farm home. The first thing I noticed was that her appearance was vastly different from what I expected. Vastly better than I anticipated. And in an impulsive moment I asked if she would like to accompany me to a movie in Fargo that evening. She said yes and we spent the evening talking about farming, athletics, and what she was doing in her work. I discovered she was an X-ray tech employed by the hospital in Fergus Falls. Oh, I think we went to a movie! If I were a fish I think I had swallowed the hook.

The next few weeks went by in a haze of activity. I became acquainted with her family, actually re-acquainted with Bud. We had played on the same Junior Legion baseball team and as opponents in basketball. Betty was about the tallest one in the family. I soon asked her to marry me and she accepted! I already knew the family had accepted me because a carpenter had been employed to enlarge the door going into the kitchen! That is, raise the entrance so I didn't have to stoop when I entered the room. I was six feet five on one leg and six feet two on the other. We agreed on December 22, 1961 as our wedding day. We had our work schedules to consider. Also there were two other teachers in the wedding party and several more as invited guests.

The day of the wedding began as a typical North Dakota December day. I drove the 35 miles to Valley City to pick up the flowers in a ground blizzard (35 miles) but when I began my return the wind had increased greatly. Soon I was forced to drive with my head out the window to see the white line in the middle of the road. After what seemed like hours I drove into the Michaelson farm yard. Inside the house I found Betty and her mother distraught wondering if the wedding should go forward. I felt the wedding should go forward because of the difficulty of re - scheduling. Fortunately the wind receded as the evening for the wedding approached.

The wedding ceremony was performed by not one but two pastors. Pastor Berg from the Hannaford church and Pastor Erberg from the Eidfjord Church. (We needed all the spiritual power we could get because I am writing this report after 49 years of marriage to the same woman). As we exchanged our vows I was humbled by the realization that I was marrying a great and beautiful girl. A brief reception was held after the wedding and then we returned to the Michaelson house where many more guests were to view the opening of the wedding gifts. That process continued until midnight. I reminded Betty that we were scheduled to leave for our honeymoon. At about one in the morning we started a trip which was planned to take us to Detroit Lakes.

The romance of the night quickly dissipated as we discovered that the road was covered by a thick coat of very slippery ice. Three hours gripping the steering wheel of the car followed until we quit and pulled into a West Fargo motel. I tease my wife that I will never forget the year 1961 as the year of our marriage because Roger Maris hit 61 home runs that year. Actually the truth is that I will never forget the death grip that I had on the wheel of our car on the night we began our honeymoon. What I thought would be a difficult adjustment time instead was quite pleasant. I began to understand the biblical term "one flesh." Some days did provide times when we acted like sand paper rubbing sand paper but those times were brief.

Chapter 5

THE MIRACLE WORKER

One winter day in 1963 it was time to receive my Masters degree in history from the University of North Dakota in Grand Forks. Betty was pregnant with Naomi and she was due to deliver in two weeks. Betty did not want to miss the ceremony at the University and she believed she would have no difficulty riding the 90 miles to attend. The vehicle we were driving was a Chevrolet station wagon although not new was quite trustworthy. We had invited both our sets of parents and we looked forward to making a day of it. We started a bit late and although it was cold in the car I expected the heater to begin to function soon. As the time passed the heat did not come on and Betty was cold but if we stopped we would miss the ceremony. She let me know how angry she was because I had not checked the car before we left. I responded that I didn't think it was as cold as she was saying. When we finally arrived at our destination a jar of milk that she placed by her foot was frozen solid. Now I was in trouble with her and both sets of parents! Someone suggested that the antifreeze might be low causing the problem so I had it checked and it solved the problem when more was added. We decided to visit my sister in Moorhead on our way home. We visited briefly and continued on our way. Before we left we agreed that Betty should drive the remaining miles because I had forgotten to renew my Minnesota driver's license. With perhaps fifteen miles from home the day had become night.

A car with its lights on was approaching us when I noticed it was drifting toward the ditch. I sat up straight and began to say "look. . ." when suddenly the car over corrected and shot across the road right at us. I only had time to lunge at the steering wheel. The impact forced the left front wheel into the engine compartment and crushed the front of our car. The other car spun down the road and came to rest in the ditch. Within our car the impact caused her to fly over me but my body protected her from being forced against the steering wheel. Her head struck the windshield and forced it out of its place. The glass was crushed where her head contacted it. She said her head hurt a bit but otherwise claimed she was unhurt. I was unhurt also. Praise the Lord! Our car had come to rest in the middle of the road and persons who had stopped were successfully directing traffic so no further accidents would occur. When the police arrived they became agitated when they realized that Betty was 9 months pregnant. We were hurried on to the doctor in Lake Park and eventually declared uninjured. When I had time to evaluate what had happened I realized we had been miraculously spared. Two weeks later the miracle continued with the birth of our daughter Naomi.

Chapter 6

"The SWORD OF THE SPIRIT"
(A Strange Place for an Introduction!)

School teaching continued for me. Naomi continued to grow. Supt. Mjolsness resigned his Lake Park position and moved to Elbow Lake to fill that vacancy. We were church attending people. Most of our friends also attended the same Lutheran church. The choir director was the music director from school. Betty and I both sang in the church choir and he was my fishing buddy, several friends including the music director also played basketball on the town team. One day we asked the Pastor to visit our apartment for coffee. It was near Halloween and he and his wife appeared. While we were visiting I jokingly said I was happy this year because this was the first year I had my own witch! Betty let me know that was not an appropriate place for that joke. These were good times and we probably would be living there yet. Then I received a phone call.

Elbow Lake was the county seat of Grant County. It was a larger town and I was promised a pay raise. I soon discovered that the music man and coach received similar calls. We were back in a happy group. The school was larger but my classroom was in the oldest part of the building. The students were a pleasure to work with and the year went quickly. The excitement of the year was provided by Tom our second baby born in March of 1965. He would be the beginning of many family adventures.

One of the requirements of the history masters program at the University of North Dakota had been to research and writes a thesis. I chose to write mine titled A HISTORY OF FARM MORTGAGE INDEBTEDNESS IN NORTH DAKOTA FROM 1920 to 1950. When it was complete I noticed one or two interesting trends. One such trend appeared when placed on a graph. It showed that despite local and worldwide economic conditions and temporary slowing the price of good farm land continued a steady price increase over a long time period. From that finding I concluded that a person who acquired such land would acquire a significant gain merely by retaining title to a farm property. With that conclusion in mind I began to seek a farm land property. The problem that prevented such an acquisition was money. Commodity farm prices were very low in the 1960s which made a lot of land available but credit was also difficult to obtain.

Nevertheless I watched for an opportunity to obtain a property. I received frequent notices from realtors throughout the state of Minnesota but none which would fit my needs.

One day I received a notice of farm property located about one hundred miles North of Elbow Lake with what I thought listed farm land at ridiculously low prices. A friend of mine with similar interests and I arranged to drive to Erskine where the realtor had his office. The realtor was an ambitious former farmer who showed us two or three places. One farm I found very interesting. It was a quarter section of flat land (160 acres) with about 90 acres being farmed and the balance in woods with a small stream running through it. All of that including a small (18 feet square house which a bachelor had recently used as his home} for a total price of $5500. If I was ever to become a land owner I told Betty when I returned from the trip it would have to be with that land. I made an offer of about 10 per cent down and a monthly payment of $60. The owner accepted the terms. I borrowed against my life insurance and the $60 dollar monthly payments were paid from my teaching salary.

The first year I discovered it was nearly impossible to find a renter for the land at any price. We made a family vacation out of living in our small house at the farm. We acquired some furniture which our families had no more use for, kept the lawn mowed and prepared the farm yard for a longer stay the next summer.

The next year of teaching went quickly. It seemed to pass quickly because my spare time was partly spent solving the problem of not being able to find a renter for our newly acquired farm land. The solution was for me to obtain machinery and farm the land myself. Several of our North Dakota friends helped us with cast off farm equipment. A tractor, combine, and various tillage tools were transported to the farm in time for the spring seeding. An old Ford pickup truck was also acquired. The equipment might be best described as antique. I carefully planned each move before I arrived at the farm so I made no movements that would delay the time available. I planned a drive to the farm on a Friday evening, work preparing the land for planting and return on Sunday night. The following week end I would repeat the process for planting. The summer that followed I moved the family to the farm for the summer. When the wheat and barley crops matured I harvested the crop, picked the garden vegetables, loaded everything in the truck and retuned to our Elbow Lake home. It was a lot of work for Betty and me but we had a wonderful time. Surprisingly it worked.

The spring of 1967 marked the third year of teaching at Elbow Lake. It also ended my tenth year of teaching. I was aware that teaching on that level also required a high degree of parenting. Although that phase of teaching was rewarding I was growing increasingly restless. My decision was already complete. I had confided in a few friends that I was going to return to law school to complete the last two years. God hadn't been consulted however, and unforeseen events began to appear on the horizon.

I had become active in the Minnesota Education Association and I was serving as the Vice President of the western division of teachers. The President of the division was a teacher at the community college in Fergus Falls, Minnesota named Carrol Crouch. One day while visiting with him I mentioned that I was ready for a change. He told me that the college was looking for a person to fill a position in history. He said "why don't you stop by and visit with the president about the position?" I hadn't thought of going that direction in my career but I was interested enough to discuss the idea with the head of the college. I met with him and when I left his office he had offered me the job. I learned that the college was very young and it did not even have a campus. But it had recently become a part of the state school system and the building of a campus was underway. In the meantime the school was located in the State hospital. It appealed to me as a place where I could do more teaching and less parenting. It also appealed to me because we could continue living where we were and the salary was considerably better. It was unanimous. We voted to give it a try. Twenty four years later I still considered it a good decision when I retired.

In May of 1968 Rebecca arrived and we now had three children to take to the farm. The farm had electricity but no water. The water had to be hauled from one of our farm neighbor friends in a plastic garbage can. That situation caused having a tiny baby with us especially difficult. Betty had the pioneer spirit and she organized the entire family to share the load. The Bernards, our realtor friends, had helped our adventure by occasionally mowing our lawn and keeping us informed of any news of the area which could be helpful. Our small house became increasingly livable as we hauled in a cupboard and an electric stove. A piece of plywood placed on six concrete blocks served as our personal and dish washing area. It also served as the place of our food preparation. A small table and an ancient cupboard completed the kitchen area. The remaining area contained a small bed and a very small sofa.

A dairy farm located a few miles east of our farm became the regular source of our water supply. It was owned by a man named Truman Rolf his wife and young family. We frequently visited with them in the evenings when the work was done. They provided much needed advice and when they learned we had no way to haul our grain to market they provided a very large trailer. Many times in later years when I thought of someone who shined with the inner light of Jesus I thought of Truman Rolf.

Some days at the farm had a long term impact on our family. One Sunday we visited the Bernard family much of the day. When we returned to our house late in the day we discovered a note pinned on our door. A neighbor sought to buy some hay from us. We decided to drive to his farm right away to sell the hay. One of the first things we had noticed when we started living at our farm was a small rural Lutheran church about a mile East of our farm. It appeared to be like most rural churches with one major difference. It was frequently surrounded by large numbers of parked cars. We attended an occasional Sunday service there and noticed it was uncommonly friendly but otherwise nothing that would account for the large number of cars.

When we arrived at the farm home of the man who wanted the hay we discovered a large farm yard covered with parked cars. We knocked on the door and the wife of the farmer answered the knock. She informed us that a prayer meeting was in progress and wouldn't we join them? We agreed and joined the large group seated in the living room. During a break in the activity one of the ladies leaned over to Betty and asked "have you been baptized in the Holy Spirit?" She thought for a moment and replied "yes" She and I had both been water baptized as babies and then had been confirmed in that decision as teenagers. No further comment followed but we pondered that question many times as we returned to our farm.

INTERMISSION

Chapter 7
THE BAPTISIM OF THE HOLY SPIRIT
(The Search)

But the Counselor, The Holy Spirit
whom the father will send in my name,
Will teach you all things and will remind
you of everything I have said to you.
John 14:26

The Lutheran Church of my youth like many protestant churches was traditional and often liturgical. The Bible was the subject of reverence but seldom opened in private homes. The Jesus proclaimed from the pulpit was often portrayed as a historical phenomenon. Hymns were often sung about and not "to" God. The Holy Spirit was named but his role was not defined. Then in the 1960s various people and some congregations began to display different manifestations that seemed to many as being super natural. Throughout the nation stories multiplied until it seemed like a giant wave was sweeping the nation. The wave was identified as the Holy Spirit. The wave grew wider and swept people through the 1960s into the 1970s and beyond... This narrative follows the wave and its impact.

One day while Betty and I along with Naomi and Tom were in Moorhead, we made the decision to visit the Mark Nielsens. We had been neighbors in Elbow Lake and together had studied a book on the Holy Spirit. When we walked into their house we realized that we had happened on a very unhappy situation. We learned that their 5 year old son Jonathon had been running through the alley behind their house when a milk truck ran over him and he had been killed. Very sad! We returned for the funeral. Three or four years then elapsed before we visited with them again. In the years between I moved to one of the three buildings on the new college campus. We continued to live in the farm house near Elbow Lake and I drove daily to the college. Naomi started school but soon had to get used to a new school because we moved to a whole new house and community.in the fall of 1969.

Elbow Lake was a difficult place to leave. The people were wonderful. The drive every day was not wonderful. We began to look for a place to live in Fergus Falls. We discovered a development with a lot that appealed to us on the Ottertail River. I sought a loan that would allow us to build a house which we felt would suit our needs. Banks that I contacted did not agree with our plans for various reasons. We had almost given up hope when I contacted the First National Bank. I showed the head of the bank our house plan, the lot we had chosen and our need for $20,000. Then I braced myself for the routine rejection. He leaned back in his chair and said "O.K." I looked at him and said "O.K." what? He smiled and said "go ahead and build." I drove home and we rejoiced that we had found a kind man who had confidence in us at last.

The house plan we had chosen was one with a walk out basement. It had a double garage and three bed rooms; we hired a carpenter from Ashby and local plumbers and electricians. The painting we would do ourselves. The oversight was my concern and it all happened within a reasonable schedule. The schedule success was especially important because the crop had to be planted and harvested at the farm within the same time frame. It was very hard work at times but the excitement of a new house at the end of the time frame made it worthwhile. The daily drive from Elbow Lake ended, the school bus transported the local kids to school, the college continued, the farm work was complete for another year and all was well with the world.

Then Jerry Bernard, our realtor friend who sold us the farm, called and said "I have a buyer for your farm." My first thought was to turn down the opportunity and then the long hard drives, the financial drain on our finances and the time drain began to shout in my sub conscious mind. I tried the idea out on the family and I realized no one complained. I would benefit very little financially but it would diminish the stress. I gave the order to sell. Later when the realization set in the whole family began to recall the many good times and we all shed many tears.

More time passed and one day as we were visiting in Moorehead it occurred to us that it had been years since we had visited the Mark Nielsens. We arrived at their house in the evening and rang the doorbell. The atmosphere that greeted us was much different from the day we learned that their son Jonathon had been killed. The Nielsen's greeted us warmly and we traded our family happenings since the last time we had visited. They recounted that their present joyful attitude was because of a meeting they had just returned from attending. It was a prayer meeting with a group they had recently come to enjoy. They recounted that a visiting evangelist had spoken and afterward had prayed for people with physical needs. They had seen miracles including the lengthening of arms and legs of people suffering from problems related to those defects.

They then recounted that in the depressed times following the death of their son they had attended a meeting of a Lutheran evangelist named Herb Mjorud. He taught that the bible contained information about the Holy Spirit of God in which those who sought to further the kingdom of God needed to be filled or baptized with the Holy Spirit. They had gone forward to answer the call to be "baptized" with the Holy Spirit. They had experienced a rush of new experiences in the days that followed and they were anxious to share those experiences. Soon we were also involved.

Mark looked at me and said "you have a short leg don't you?" I replied that I did because of a serious accident when I was eleven years old. He then invited me to sit down in a nearby chair. He said he would pray for my leg to lengthen and it would "come right out." I said "ok" but inwardly I was thinking "I don't believe it." I sat in the chair and extended my shorter leg. He did not grab my foot and give it a jerk. Instead he merely rested the heel of my foot on his open hand and began to pray. After a short time nothing appeared to be happening. He then began to pray in tongues I had never heard that before. Still nothing happened. The sweat began appearing on his forehead but still nothing happened. Then he stopped praying and quietly mentioned "it must not be in his timing."

He then turned to Betty and asked her "do you have a short leg?" I thought to myself what great tenacity! Surprisingly she had recently visited a doctor because she was suffering from back pain. He had measured her legs and discovered that one of her legs was three quarters of an inch shorter than the other. He motioned to her to sit in the same chair I had just vacated. He held her extended leg in the same way he had held my foot and began to pray. I thought to myself if anything is going to happen I want to see this. I stationed my head about 12 inches above her leg so I could clearly see any change. Almost before I was in position Betty grabbed her leg and exclaimed "what's happening?" What I witnessed was the leg acting like an earth worm extending itself as it moved along. Unquestionably the leg had lengthened. Betty and I expressed our amazement.

We visited about miracles, about the Baptism of the Spirit, and then we drove the 60 miles to our home. On the way we visited more about our feelings of the events. Betty was exhilarated by the lengthening of her leg. I found my feelings to be one of depression. As I searched my mind for why I should have reacted in that way I came to realize that I had come to believe that God loved her but not me or he would have lengthened my leg also. Could it have been because of my hospital accusation of God that he had allowed my injury? I wrestled that thought out of my conscious mind and resolved to search the scriptures to learn more about what Mark had experienced.

Reality returned with our return home that evening. Tom appeared to have the flu. We were scheduled to attend a hay ride for young people that evening from the Lutheran Church we had joined in Fergus Falls. I said I would stay home with Tom and she should go to the hay ride. She attended but afterward a friend approached her and asked "what is the matter with Paul I saw him coming out of church this morning and he was limping." She immediately realized that if she told what we had experienced that day that she would be placed in a box with people who had pretty wild ideas if not sick ideas. She realized that she better think before saying anything so she said nothing.

As time allowed I began the search which I hoped would lead me to the truth of what Mark and his wife had experienced. I began by taking stock of what I already thought I knew. I thought I knew quite a lot about the Bible. I had attended a college with a religious emphasis. I had many credit hours in the study of religious subjects. I had attended a steady diet of chapel services almost daily for four years. I knew virtually nothing about the Holy Spirit and with all my other knowledge it added up to the need to start from scratch. I soon realized that I had more questions than answers and so with the questions I began with the one that was key to many others.

Question one: After being a Christian all these years why didn't I know more about this person of God? The classic answer was the commonly accepted belief that the gifts of the Holy Spirit mentioned in various places in the Bible were a dispensation by God which disappeared with the passing of the early church. The evidence for that was not apparent to me anywhere in the Bible so I rejected it. I also concluded from experience that there was a wall of ridicule for anyone that put forth personal experiences or teachings that appeared to be "super natural."

Question two: Is there more than one baptism? I thought I had been baptized once for all. I had been baptized as a baby and confirmed as a teen. The words used were from Matt. 18:19 *"in the name of the Father, the Son, and of the Holy Spirit."* They appear to be one. Nevertheless, in Mark 1:4 John preached and performed a baptism for the forgiveness of sins. Jesus next came to John and asked him to baptize him despite the fact he was God man. In the process of the baptism a dove descended on Jesus as a symbol of the Holy Spirit coming upon him while God the Father spoke his approval. John is then heard to say to an observer *"I baptize you with water but he will baptize you with the Holy Spirit."* Jesus soon began his ministry which to that time he had not begun. Jesus had laid aside his God power when he had entered the world as a mortal man. The sign that he had resumed God power apparently was the baptism of the Holy Spirit performed by John the Baptist. During his ministry Jesus performed miracles, cast out demons, and Mark 4:23 *"healed every disease and sickness among the people.*" In John 14:12 Jesus proclaims "I tell you the truth, anyone who has faith in me will do what I have been doing. He will do even greater things than these because I am going to the Father." These events indicated to me that the power of God is transmitted by a baptismal act to Jesus and that other persons would also be baptized with the same power. Apparently my friend Mark and his wife were some of those persons. The prophet Joel (Chapter 2) and the prophet Jeremiah (Chapter 31) both wrote that the Holy Spirit would be sent into the world and he would play a mighty role in God's plan of salvation.

Question three: What is the role of the Holy Spirit in the world? When Jesus had been crucified and resurrected he spoke to his disciples as he was about to ascend to be with the Father. He said Luke 11:11-13"I am going to send you what my Father has promised but stay in the city until you have been clothed with power from on high." Jesus did not want the disciples to begin the work of building the body of Christ (the Church) until they were filled or clothed with the "power" to do the job in the way God wanted it built. Acts 1:8. That answers the primary role of the Holy Spirit. How he would build the church would be to call people to Jesus through the gospel. When they accepted Jesus as their Savior he would take up residency in their temple (their body). Their Spirit would then be guided by the Holy Spirit within them and they would be said to be born again. The Holy Spirit becomes a kind of compass in which the person is counseled, comforted and convicted of sin. (John, Chapters 14 and 16) The person then may be said to be with the Holy Spirit when unsaved. When born again the Holy Spirit changes his position to be in the saved person, and for those who desire to help build the body of Christ the person will receive "power" when the Holy Spirit comes "upon" them. The lengthening of Betty's leg was the power of God "witnessing" through Mark Nielsen. These questions and answers were not as clear as they seem when stated here but they were clear enough at the time for me to conclude that without the understanding and the power of the Holy Spirit I was like a soldier without a gun!

The question of how to receive my gun seemed more complex than the previous ones. Again I searched the scriptures and talked to people who had experienced the infilling of the Holy Spirit. Some had "hands laid on them." Some seemed to have received when they were born again. Others when they were receiving ministry. Some received in groups, others while deep in solitary prayer. Some had a rush of emotional activity and immediately spoke in tongues. Others didn't have an emotional experience and if they spoke in tongues it was later. One method which seemed common to many was explained in Luke Chapter eleven. They "asked."

Chapter eleven opens with a disciple of Jesus saying "Lord, teach us to pray." He responds by instructing them to pray much of the Lord's Prayer. Then almost like changing the subject Jesus tells a story of a man who approaches a friend to obtain food for another friend who had arrived at night while on a journey. At first the friend refuses the request but with persistent knocking at the door the friend gives him what he needs. The lesson taught by the story was to be bold or persistent in prayer and rest in the assurance that God answers prayer. With that lesson Jesus continues in verses 9, 10 "So I say to you: ask and it will be given to you; seek and you will find; knock and the door will be opened to you. For everyone who asks receives; he who seeks finds; and to him who knocks the door will be opened."

These illustrations say be bold and "ask" for we are assured that God answers prayers. Therefore ask to receive the infilling of the Holy Spirit for you are assured that you will receive what you ask. Then to reinforce the assurance he says "Which of you fathers, if your son asks for a fish, will give him a snake instead? Or if he asks for an egg, will give him a scorpion? If you then, though you are evil, know how to give good gifts to your children, how much more will your Father in heaven give the Holy Spirit to those who ask him?" Notice that the illustration specifically refers to the Holy Spirit.

As I meditated on this bit of God's word I resolved to accept this knowledge as revelation and although others may have received the infilling of the Holy Spirit in different ways who was I to limit the power of God. At no time did I believe that I had to get filled with the Holy Spirit to be saved. I was saved. I had been born again of the Spirit when I accepted what Jesus had done for my salvation at the cross. Instead I sought to receive all the power that he had for me for his purposes. I had very few ideas what those purposes would be or when they would be needed.

Often times when I prayed to God I quickly forgot when and what I had prayed. This prayer was different. I was determined to remember when, where and what I had prayed in asking for the Holy Spirit to come upon me in power. On the fourth of July, a day hard to forget, I happened to be driving our car by myself on the way to my Uncle Albert's lake cabin where a reunion of mine and several other families were meeting. It was an ideal time to ask. It was a simple prayer. I began by telling the Lord that I didn't know whether I should ask to be filled with the Holy Spirit or baptized with the Holy Spirit but "just do it!" I felt no different. The only difference I noticed was that I was absolutely convinced that if I asked my earthly father for a good gift he would not simply ignore me or hand me a skunk. Then I thought to myself that I probably should now be able to speak in tongues so I made some sounds with my mouth and thought to myself if anyone asks me now I can say to them that I have been filled with the

Spirit and I speak in tongues. With that I continued my drive, enjoyed the reunion and put the whole thing out of my mind! Two weeks passed and it was Sunday the day Betty and I met with three other couples for a bible study. All of us were members of the Bethlehem Lutheran church. That evening our discussion had drifted away from anything remotely related to the Bible. I became aware that we were wandering and I had an intense inner feeling that I should bring the discussion back to things spiritual. The intense feeling next arose to the pitch best described as a volcano! I began to speak in the manner of a "side show barker" about spiritual subjects. The harangue continued with my wife who was seated near me reaching with her foot to kick me so that she could motion for me to sit down and shut up. After a while the "volcano" subsided, I sat down and apologized profusely. I said I didn't know what had come over me but it certainly wouldn't happen again. The evening ended with a time of coffee and conversation and a bit of teasing about my preaching ability. When two weeks had passed our Bible study group met again. Midway through the evening I resumed preaching while my wife continued her kicking and motioning for me to stop and be quiet. After a time I had said my thoughts and stopped much to Betty's relief. Again I apologized and repeated that would not happen again. This time, however, I began to realize that my request to be filled with the Holy Spirit had been fulfilled! Now I thought "what would be next?"

Chapter 8

LETTING GO LETTING GOD
(IN THE HOLY SPIRIT)

A s a teacher at the college I thought it was my responsibility to share my experience with the church by teaching an adult class. I had been teaching it for a year or two with limited success. The attendance was easy to tabulate because although there was about two thousand confirmed members in the church the number of adults in my class averaged between four and eight. It is true that the conditions for attending an adult class were not ideal. Several classes of all ages shared the basement area of the church. The conditions were just short of being described as bedlam and it was difficult to hear anyone without elevating ones voice. Nevertheless, an average attendance of four out of two thousand was lamentable.

A Snapshot: Bob Torkelson is seated on a stool. He is not very tall and an accordion on his lap nearly hides his entire body. He is a former owner of a music store where he had given accordion lessons. After the sale of his store he became a real estate sales person where he was equally skilled. Beside him is his wife Ruby. Together they were baptized in the Holy Spirit and were on fire for the Lord.

One Sunday after completing a class under "lamentable" conditions I spoke to the sixth grade teacher whose class occupied the space adjacent to mine. I later learned that he had recently been filled with the Holy Spirit and was anxious to improve the learning conditions also. As we visited I asked him if he would be interested in inviting a few adults to my class of adults and I would invite a few people also. I would teach the book of John verse by verse and we would see if the Sunday school conditions would improve. He agreed to help. We acquired a little larger area in the basement and the first Sunday we met fifteen adults joined the class. I opened the book of John to the first verse of chapter one. I read the first verse and asked the question "is there anyone that does not understand what that says?" "O K" I said and I repeated the same question for verse number two. In that way the class continued until the end of the hour. At the end of the hour Bob Torkelson, the sixth grade teacher, and I met and agreed that it was a success and we would continue the same pattern.

Two weeks later I was teaching seventy adults. Two or three situations were becoming apparent at the same time that the numbers were increasing. The people were contributing to the class and some were demonstrating strong emotion in the process. The second situation was that a large number of people that attended were not members of Bethlehem church. They were people who heard that there was an exciting class happening in the basement of Bethlehem church and they were coming in the front door, walking to the basement, attending the class and then without attending the worship services they exited the church to reappear the following Sunday. Pastor Jim, the head pastor at Bethlehem, gradually became aware with increased numbers attending the adult class that something was happening but he didn't appear alarmed. As time continued some class members asked if I would also teach on Sunday evening and I agreed. More time passed and I was asked if I would teach one evening during the week as well. I agreed.

With the increased activity Pastor Jim now invited me to his office where he asked me a number of questions. One good question he asked of me was "why aren't the class members coming to Bethlehem Church services?" I wasn't sure why all were coming but one dominant reason I felt was due to the efforts of the Holy Spirit. Another question was "Where and when are you getting all of the stuff you are teaching?" I replied, "Well usually I get the best stuff in bed about six in the morning the day I am scheduled to teach." I didn't intend the answer to be flippant. I merely meant that I would read over what I would teach next. I would then awaken in the morning and meditate on what I had read the night before. The meditation would lead to what I would teach. I felt I was experiencing my own thought process in my times of meditation. As time went on, however, I began to realize that those thoughts were often aided by the Holy Spirit. Later I would learn to depend fully on John 14:26 which I memorized from the NIV version of the bible which states "but the counselor whom the Father will send in my name, he will teach you all things and will remind you of everything I have said to you."

Pastor Jim had many fine Pastoral qualities. Many of those qualities had been perfected at the Lutheran seminary he attended. The seminary was liturgical and traditional. Therefore, Pastor Jim protected the liturgical and the traditional way of pastoring a church. The Holy Spirit was identified but not fully understood.

One Sunday evening about 45 class members came to a session I was teaching in an upstairs room of the church. After teaching three times a week verse by verse we had advanced through the books of John, Acts, Romans, and were midway through the book of First Corinthians. The Apostle Paul was the author of the book or letter to the Corinthians. He was concerned about several practices of the church which had become misinterpreted and he used the letter to correct their understandings. Because I had been filled with the Holy Spirit I had read Chapters twelve, thirteen, and fourteen in which Paul had dealt with those imperfect practices. I was anxious to teach the chapters not only for the class but also for my personal insight.

Paul begins Chapter 12 with the words "now about Spiritual gifts, brothers, I do not want you to be ignorant." He then follows with nine ways the Holy Spirit manifests himself within the Body of Christ. Each are defined and encouraged to be used in the manner that each person has been gifted. They are to be used as tools like a carpenter would use a hammer or saw. Where a carpenter would build a house a gifted person would build the church in the way the Holy Spirit wants it built.

The term "ignorance of Spiritual gifts" appeared to me to be a command to be careful not to remain ignoring them. Ignoring the gifts is to limit the role of the Holy Spirit. It is contrary to the very strong words of Paul. It would seem that the modern church is risking a sin against the Holy Spirit by claiming that the gifts were for another age. Paul is using strong words to say listen to the word of God. I wondered what Jesus would say about a similar attitude. Although an illustration by Jesus to the Pharisees is not quite the same he replies to their question of why his disciples don't wash their hands before they eat by telling them they have the command to honor their father and mother but twist the meaning to nullify the Word of God for the sake of their tradition. (Matt. 15:1-7)

The gifts or manifestations of the Spirit (nine in number) are listed in chapter 12 of First Corinthians. While discussing them in the class it was evident that we shared some ignorance. One misunderstanding common to many was the word "prophecy." The idea that prophecy is limited to knowledge of future events is partly right. It also is understood as "forth telling" or speaking out such as preaching the Word. Another ignorance was the term "speaking in tongues." Or "interpreting tongues" I did not speak in tongues at that time so although we read the Bible description we needed to observe the phenomenon for ourselves. I knew a local lady who had been raised a Pentecostal Christian. I had contacted her and she was present at the evening session. Midway through our meeting I introduced her and asked her if she would demonstrate. I already knew she spoke in tongues and she had already agreed. She spoke in tongues for a minute or two. And then Ruby, Bob's wife who also had been filled with the Spirit stood to her feet and put both hands to her neck and said "what's happening?" "What's happening?" A blackboard in back of me was in front of Ruby. With her hands still around her neck she began to read line after line from the blackboard which only she could see! To me it sounded similar to a psalm but we were all startled and not ready to listen to an interpretation of the tongue. Besides a lady was standing in the back of the room saying that while she was speaking in tongues she had been praying that someone would interpret. We had received more than what we bargained for and for the next few minutes there wasn't much doubt about the presence of the Holy Spirit in our midst and we had observed the super natural first hand. The Holy Spirit had just demonstrated the same action as that recorded in First Corinthians Chap. 12. And it was in the 20th century, not the first century!

Oh my! Until this time the teaching was acceptable to Lutheran theology. The word spread quickly that speaking in tongues was occurring in the adult class. The assistant pastor frequently attended the class and I was invited to come to Pastor Jim's office during the week to discuss what had been taught that week. Bob Torkelson received similar invitations.

I continued teaching First Corinthians Chapter 12, 13, and 14. One of the questions that lingered was "is it necessary for a Christian to speak in tongues? My response was "no" but you have the opportunity to do so. Then the next question was "why, what is the purpose?" My reply was to read from First Corinthians 14: 4 and 5. "He who speaks in a tongue edifies himself, but he who prophesies edifies the church. I would like every one of you to speak in tongues, but I would rather have you prophesy. He who prophesies is greater than one who speaks in tongues, unless he interprets, so that the church may be edified." We noticed the difference between speaking alone or in the church. Also a difference between tongues and prophesy. Prophesy appears to be most important because it builds the church unless within the church tongues are combined with interpretation so all can understand. Finally the answer to the question "why tongues" is so the individual speaking may be built up. (My personal opinion is that tongues are a gateway to the exercise of the rest of the Spirit gifts. As you are built up you discover that you can function in areas previously unknown) so that you may witness more effectively.

Finally we turned our attention to Chapter 13. First the importance of the chapter is stressed in the last verse of Chapter 12. "And now I will show you the most excellent way." In brief: The use of gifts without love is less useful.

An apple tree grows for a long time before it bears apples (fruit) so too is the Christian. Time following Jesus in the Holy Spirit results in fruit. I think of Truman Rolt the kind and love filled man near our farm when we needed a wagon or water. He shined with Jesus love. It was the most perfect witness. It is no mistake that chapter 13 is between chapters

12 and 14. The gun of a Christian is most well-armed with both the gifts and love.

Pastor Jim now had a problem. Functioning in the gifts seems to put Satan's opposition into high gear. Persons in the congregation now began to talk about the tongue talking people in that class. Sides began to form and I also had a problem. If I continued the class I probably would split the church. If I stopped the potential revival of the church might end, or if I continued the revival an effective church might end. My decision was to notify Pastor Jim that I would be leaving Bethlehem Lutheran Church. The word of my leaving soon spread and several persons contacted me. They urged me to stay but I told them I did not want to split the church. Then others urged me to find another place to teach and suggested that I use my classroom at the College where I taught history every school day. The room seated 96 so that would be fine but they would have to contact the college president for permission to use the room for a religious purpose. I already reasoned that would not be possible because of the separation of church and state. The answer showed how little I still understood about the workings of the Holy Spirit. President Waage said "sure, go ahead" and I thought "now what?"

Chapter 9

THE HOLY SPIRIT BIRTHS
A CHURCH

On a Sunday morning a small group of people who had supported the continuation of the class beyond Bethlehem Lutheran Church assembled together at the college classroom. I taught verse by verse beginning from where I had left off in the Bible and at the end of the hour we agreed to meet continually for an indefinite time. After several weekly meetings various leaders suggested that we add a time of worship after the teaching session. That suggestion was agreed to as well as a suggestion that we remain simply a Christian group rather than accept any particular denomination. We also agreed to read and understand the words we read as they were simply stated. All appeared to be in agreement on one basic idea. The idea that the Holy Spirit was central to the building of the Christian Church on earth and that it was essential that we in our group needed to learn how to follow his lead.

The number of people in the Bible class increased during the early months of meeting together. Included in the group were Bob and Ruby Torkelson as well as many other Bethlehem Lutheran folks. Other churches were also represented including Pastor Art and Dorothy Mueller formerly of the Lutheran Brethern denomination. After about a year someone suggested that we do the necessary paper work to declare ourselves a church. Among other reasons for formally organizing was the fact that contributors could write the gift off their income tax. The government of the group followed closely that recorded in First Timothy. The elders were Art Amundson, Art Mueller and I. There were also many deacons who handled the business end of the church and the congregation usually ran well. The Elders worked with spiritual issues and the head of the elders was the hired pastor when the position was filled

One thing was quite unique and worked very well. It. was termed the "love" fund. Every contributed dollar was put in the fund at the rate of 10 per cent. That money was then distributed to any needy person whether in the church or outside the church. It worked well and the church was seldom in need. The title selected for the Church was the LORD JESUS FELLOWSHIP. Perhaps the major problem was the lack of a Covering. That meant that we had no oversight from a larger group or persons dedicated to pray protection from spiritual problems that could arise and sometimes did. We did benefit from the strength of having Pastor Art as an elder. Also the congregation had many prayer warriors who did pray regularly. Worship services often lasted about one and one half hours. Perhaps one third was music led worship and the rest was preaching and organization needs such as communion or prayer for the individual needs of the people. The gifts were also liberally sprinkled in the weekly services. Prophesy, tongues, miracles, healing, and words of knowledge were commonly displayed.

As was earlier explained, Art Mueller had conducted the meeting that the Mark Nielsens had attended shortly before we had visited their home and Betty's leg had lengthened. Art had been filled with the Spirit while attending a

Rex Humbard crusade in which he received a special gift of lengthening arms and legs. As a Lutheran brethren evangelist he added teaching on the Holy Spirit to his ministry and as a result he was removed from the Church as an evangelist but retained his ordination papers. Eventually he joined with Pastor Mjorud and the two of them preached the Baptism of the Holy Spirit with the gifts. They traveled around the world several times performing and witnessing incredible miracles among peoples. In his auto biography Pastor Mjorud recounts the raising of a woman who had died and in his own life doctors sent him home from a hospital to die. He then recounts that God spoke to him telling him to praise him for 24 hours and he would be healed. He replied to the Lord that he was too weak to praise him but his wife brought a tape player with recorded praise music. Twenty four hours later he rose from his bed completely healed!

Art also recalled several stories from his ministry. He was so well thought of in Finland that when he visited there he was front page news in the newspapers. One incident was recorded where Art was asked to bless a handkerchief which was taken to a hospital room where another woman lay dying. She was healed and immediately walked from her room. When Art was in a room where I was teaching I would call people to the front of the room to witness the miracle! I was his most notable failure. He prayed for my leg to lengthen several times but it was never successful. If the failure could be interpreted as lessoning the impact or suggesting that there was something fake involved I offer the following incident:

One evening Art held a bible study in his home. Several people attended including a woman whose name was Hittle. She had a leg six inches shorter than the other. Art and Ron Weise prayed for her leg to lengthen. Her leg lengthened two inches. The following week they prayed for the lady again and her leg lengthened two inches more. The third night after prayer her leg joined the other in length (what a great testimony that woman was given). But her witness was not to be. Hittle lived on a farm with her husband and an orphan they had chosen to raise. When the orphan reached adulthood he became involved in a serious crime and was imprisoned. His release from prison occurred shortly after Mrs. Hittle's leg was lengthened. He returned to the Hittle home where he shot and killed both Mrs. Hittle and her husband. She did not have the opportunity to witness the miracle but Dorothy, Arts wife, explained that Art carried the shoe in his car for a long time. The shoe proclaimed the miracle for a long time with Art's help.

Art served the Fellowship and the community in many ways. He served as an elder and often preached as well especially in the formative years. In the community he loved to attend auction sales. At the sales he liked to circulate on the edge of the crowd where he would begin a conversation with a person. He would look at them and ask "How do you have it with the Lord?" Then he would witness to them and move on to the next person. As an evangelist he had a personality which was opinionated and bold but those qualities often served him well when he approached unfamiliar persons.

Lord Jesus Fellowship had been organized but had not gone the next step and called a pastor. We relied on much leadership from pastor Muellor and some advice was obtained from leaders within the Lutheran Conference on the Holy Spirit. One such leader who offered his help and mentoring was pastor Rod Lensch. He was an ordained Missouri Synod Lutheran pastor who had been filled with the Spirit and found himself without support from the Synod because of what they thought was contrary to their beliefs. He had developed as a kind of pastor at large who offered his services to churches like our fellowship. He helped by providing names of pastors that we might consider the pastor of a church like ours.

Lyle Thorpe was a name that was provided. He had been hired for a series of weeks so the group could determine if he would fit into our needs. Although he had major problems in his youth and had served prison time, he had been converted and was a dynamic leader a good speaker and was married to a fine Christian woman. One Sunday he accompanied our church group to the Jesus is Lord church located in Minneapolis where we sought to learn from their experience of operating a church similar to ours. During the service my mind began to wander from the sermon because I was interested in whether Lyle Thorpe would agree to serve the fellowship as our pastor. I did not consider myself gifted as a prophet but I asked the Lord if he would serve as our pastor. Immediately I received a reply. A vision of a beautiful large apple tree appeared in my mind. As I viewed the large apples that hung from the tree one apple grew in size and fell to the ground. It then began to bounce in my direction while growing to a huge size. As it came close to me it bounced by me and continued off down the hill. I realized that it was an answer to my question but understanding the message was unclear. At the end of the service we gathered in a group and I asked Lyle if the vision meant anything to him. He pondered for a moment and then shook his head "no." As I drove home the interpretation came quickly and was almost as clear as the vision. The large apple on the tree was Lyle. As he came toward the church he was growing in his ministry. If he chose to minister at the Lord Jesus Fellowship he and the church would prosper and be very successful. But, if he passed on our church he would serve another. In fact he chose to pass on by and serve another.

The Fellowship chose a traditionally trained Lutheran pastor who served for a short period of years. The name of the pastor was Bill Moberly. He continued the church in the way that had become comfortable to the group.

After serving for about 4 years he and his family would move to another call. His leadership was a time of consolidating many practices. The major problem would be meeting in the college theatre with all the needs of the church within the bounds of the college requirements. The next pastor was already well known to the community and the church. His name was Dan Mueller, the son of Art and Dorothy Mueller.

The Church continued on in a similar pattern but was also hampered by the need to function within the requirements of the college. I wondered if he would be able to assert himself under the umbrella of his veteran father but he showed himself to be up to the task. After five years of service he moved on to the pastorate of the Jesus is Lord Church in Minneapolis in 1992.

Chapter 10

A WAVE OF THE HOLY SPIRIT
(The Lutheran Conference of the Holy Spirit; a realization that there were thousands of others in the Lutheran Church experiencing manifestations, counseling, and comfort of the Holy Spirit.)

The name chosen for the church was the Lord Jesus Fellowship but in smaller letters following the title on printed papers were the words "a charismatic church in the Lutheran tradition. This title served to separate the church from other local churches with an emphasis on the Holy Spirit. Our closest connection to other groups was one that Bob and Ruby had become aware of earlier. It was named the Lutheran conference on the Holy Spirit and it met yearly for a week in the Minneapolis Auditorium usually during the month of August. Thousands of persons who were filled with the Holy Spirit attended meetings there and visited about common interests and problems. Their goal was not to leave their Lutheran churches but to renew them.

Art Mueller had taught an occasional session there and Bob and Ruby had attended sessions there in the past. They considered it the best of all Lutheran activities. They had asked Betty and me to accompany them when I had begun Sunday school teaching at Bethlehem but we weren't ready. When they asked us again they were concerned that we would not accept the activity there but they should not have worried. When we walked into the auditorium the large stage was covered with musicians playing worship music of the type where people with raised hands were singing to God as though he was right there and enjoying the praise. I felt that I had come home. For the next several years we set those days aside and took the whole family there to enjoy coming home!

Our times at the conferences were spent listening to well-known speakers, attending teaching sessions, and visiting with others of like mind. Of course there was also shopping events, eating with other people from our church also attending the conference and learning about the workings of the Holy Spirit. We also liked to acquire hotel accommodations with others from our church so we could exchange help if needed. One night we had to leave early the next morning to attend an important family event. We bunked in with Bob, Ruby and two of their young boys. We visited late into the night even though we knew we had to leave around four o'clock in the morning. When we went to bed we continued to laugh and visit. The fact that my leg had never responded to lengthening was a subject that amused Bob who in his laughter proposed that we pray to shorten the other leg. When the laughter subsided in the quiet of the night Ruby said she felt someone's foot in her bed and claimed my leg had lengthened the several feet to their bed. After that the evening got noisier until the two young boys came and said "knock it off." They couldn't sleep and we should be ashamed. We left early in the morning thinking that attending a conference of that nature was sometimes not quite what others would expect.

The afternoons were usually times of Bible study. We discovered that they would hold our interest despite the fact they often lasted two or three hours. Some sessions had special subjects interesting to one or another. We tried to build our schedules so someone would attend that subject which was most interesting to that person and when the day ended we could share the main points covered by each.

One of the announced meetings was a healing service scheduled for the morning. The leader would be a well-known author of young person's adventure books with a Christian theme. Her name was Lois Walford Johnson and I arranged to be the person to attend that session. It met in the large central Lutheran church sanctuary adjacent to the Minneapolis auditorium where most of the other sessions met. When I arrived I found the church was crowded. Lois Johnson began the meeting by asking the entire audience to pray for the healing of people who were to come forward for Lois to lay hands on them and pray. A double line began to form in front of her and I decided to join as I could use some healing but for something of a personal nature.

By the time I joined the line it was half way down the center aisle. Soon it grew much longer and Lois Johnson began by asking the first person in the line what the physical problem was so she could pray over it. When she learned of the problem she shouted the problem to the crowded church. That method of group prayer made me uneasy because my physical problem was quite sensitive. As she prayed I noticed that two men would stand behind the person prayed for whom frequently fell to the floor as though they had been hit in the head with a hammer. I soon realized that the men behind the person prayed for caught them so they would not be injured when they encountered the floor. As I advanced to about fifth in line the entire front of the church was covered with people who looked like they were in deep sleep. I knew the condition of those on the floor was termed being "slain in the Spirit", but I had never seen such a mass number in one place at one time. At this point in line I wondered whether I should drop out of the line or tough it out to the end.

I had noticed that two or three persons had whispered their problem to Lois Johnson and she had turned to the side and motioned to a woman and she had led the person out of the line to a side room. As I sweat my way to the position where I could tell her my reason for healing I told her that the reason for healing was private. Again she motioned to the woman who came and directed me to follow her. Things were going to be better I thought. We moved to the kneeling rail in the front of the church and we both kneeled. At that moment she leaned over and asked me the way she should pray for me. The somewhat hallowed moment was broken completely because when she asked me the question she breathed on me and her breath was offensive beyond description! I tried to listen as she prayed a fine prayer but it was very difficult. Then without expecting it I began to weep uncontrollably. When she ended her prayer she stood and moved back to the area of the slain. The weeping continued so violently I had to stumble my way to the hallway that ran around the edge of the sanctuary. Eventually I was able to control the weeping and return to meet my wife and our friends. In later sessions I discovered that when I sought to worship I would experience additional weeping. In my thoughts I concluded that the Holy Spirit had made his presence known.

Each time we attended the Lutheran Conference on the Holy Spirit in succeeding years it seemed some new adventure awaited me or some other member of our group. In one of the last conferences we attended in the Minneapolis auditorium before it was demolished and replaced an incredible experience that I was not ready for occurred. For some time Betty had complained that although she had frequently asked to be filled with the Holy Spirit she had never received an answer to her request. At that time when I read "ask, seek and knock" I believed that the Holy Spirit would complete all the steps when the ask portion was complete. Ignored was the command to "seek and knock" for then the door will be opened to you. Of course that presented another problem. How do you seek? My understanding of that was "go where he may be found." To me it seemed that place would be where others were manifesting the gifts of the Spirit. When that command was complete the specific request (knock) could be made and the door would be opened.

Despite my limited understanding of what the word meant I decided that when we attended the next conference I would fast and pray for her to receive the baptism. As the week arrived I began a pattern of prayer in which I had eight places where I had inserted markers in my bible that said when you ask you will receive. As I progressed through the week I continually reminded God of his written word which promised that asking would be followed by receiving and for him to "protect his word." As the week wore on I received no answer. Finally on the last day I knew there was to be a time when persons who sought the baptism of the Holy Spirit were to come forward to the stage where persons were available to lay hands on them for the purpose of obtaining the baptism of the Holy Spirit in power. The auditorium was filled that evening with thousands of people. Betty was absent. She had stopped in the gift shop and had not yet arrived. Meanwhile I was desperately going over the bible passages and ending the prayers with the words "protect your word." The persons on the stage also continued to call for people to come forward while I eagerly watched the entrance to the auditorium but without her appearance. Almost miraculously she appeared and advanced to the seat on the bleachers in front of me. Bob and Ruby occupied the seats beside me and the seat she sat in was the only one left available. I continued to desperately pray. Finally she arose from her seat and moved toward the stage. I understood that to mean that my prayer request was about to be answered and in a great feeling of thanksgiving I raised my arms and began to praise God! Suddenly I felt two hands had grasped me around my waste and I experienced what could best be described as a WHOOSH. Immediately I realized that I was seated on the lap of a very large individual. The lap was big enough to make me feel like a young child! The neck and head of what appeared to be a man was not visible. It appeared to be covered by a cloud. Below the cloud was what appeared to be the very large bulk of a man clothed with a garment of a rough heavy weave? It had the appearance of a tan colored sack out of which a hole had been cut in the bottom, turned upside down with the head threaded through the hole and the remainder of the sack draped over the body from the shoulders to slightly below the knees. From the knees to sandals on the feet was what appeared to be wide strips of raw hide woven in a pattern, No word was spoken. When I took my eyes off the body I could see I looked out and down. I saw that we were suspended several hundred feet above the floor of the auditorium. The crowd was all in place and there in the bleachers were Bob and Ruby with me standing beside them with my hands raised in praise! In the brief moments that my senses processed these happenings the thought flashed through my mind that I must have died! I exclaimed "Oh no!" and half turned to push myself away from the man whose lap I was seated on and in an instant I found myself back standing in the auditorium with my hands extended in praise.

Although I tried to tell my friends what had happened, it seemed difficult to communicate the reality of the event. It was definitely not a vision. It was as real an event as any I have ever experienced in life. It was an event I have pondered frequently and one I have witnessed to others for the purpose of sharing the reality that where God resides is only a WHOOSH away. Betty eventually came to realize she too had been filled with the Holy Spirit.

One day much later I gave a hitch-hiker a ride, something I seldom did and while we traveled we visited. I asked him if he was a Christian, He said yes. Then I asked if he had been baptized in the Spirit. He replied that he had asked for that several times but with no success. That answer made me wonder how many people there were who had asked to be filled but had never sought out a person who could mentor him or help him to seek after what he had received. The word never had the opportunity to bear fruit in his life because he failed to seek what the word said he already had received.

AUTHOR COMMENT;

The Bible records few insights into heaven and heavenly events. Only a few persons in the bible experienced angels and other super natural events. The wave of the late 20th century has been accompanied by events of "out of body" and "death" experiences. The modern media has magnified these events until they have become common subjects of discussion. Are they all real and truthful experiences? Like my WHOOSH most are true. What is God's purpose of this enlightenment at this time in world history? Perhaps it is the work of the Holy Spirit for the purpose of building the church. Is this a phenomenon of the last days of the end times? These are exciting questions of speculation but not yet fully revealed.

Chapter 11

A HOLY SPIRIT DETOUR OF FAMILY HAPPENINGS

W hile these events were developing within Lord Jesus Fellowship, the Lord was also leading our family in ways we would not even imagine. One evening our family was invited to have our evening meal at the Wally Ness home our children Tom and Naomi were in high school and Becca in middle school. Their three children were similar in age so we had an enjoyable evening. While Wally and I visited he informed me that they had read an advertisement in the local newspaper in which the Lutheran Social Service had announced the need for foster parents to care for unaccompanied Vietnamese minors. They had then applied to take one boy and they had been informed that he was already on the way to their home. Wally then turned to me and said "why don't you do the same?" I quickly informed him that we were already a foster home because of parenting a mentally handicapped adult and we had ended that situation after nearly one and a half years because he was very difficult to manage. The experience of working with a Downs Syndrome person for a year had been a growing experience for our entire family. It was also an experience which had stretched us a bit beyond our abilities.

In 1973 the children were all attending Adams Elementary School in Fergus Falls. The selling of our Northern Minnesota farm had occurred three years previously and all had adjusted. Ten year old Naomi led her brother and sister on to the school bus as the eldest. Eight year old Thomas endured her oversight. Five year old Becca profited from the attention of both. Our Maltese cocker spaniel named "Boots" waited patiently for their return each day.

Betty used her new found freedom during the day to work part time with two other women at a Day Care Center for mentally handicapped adults. She could work there and return home to welcome the children when they arrived home on the bus. My income from teaching supplied our needs but we appreciated the added money from Betty's work. When we were married we had agreed to tithe to the church from our income. The additional income made it easier to keep that promise and to enjoy more financial freedom.

One day Betty returned from work to announce that one of the Downs Syndrome men needed to be placed in a foster home. In addition to the Downs Syndrome he was mildly emotionally disturbed and difficult to place. After some family discussion we decided to provide that home.

A SNAPSHOT

Verlyn Hagen is pictured sitting in a swing. He is seated with one leg hanging down from the seat of the swing while his other leg is tucked under him in a way that only those with Downs Syndrome can easily perform. He has the typical appearance of one with Downs Syndrome but one who usually has a smile on his face. He is not very tall, only about the height of our eight year old son Tom. Verlyn, however, is a little over weight. He appears to have short legs and walks a little like an upright bear...He appears to "pad along" rather than stride.

Verlyn settled into a bedroom he shared with Tom. He was able to dress himself, feed himself, visit the bathroom by himself, and to respond to those around him. Five year old Becca immediately attached herself to him and they played together on much the same level.

One of the first days after Verlyn joined our family I heard a loud sound like that of Tom pounding on his bedroom wall with a hammer. The sound reverberated throughout the house and I quickly asked Betty what was happening. Her reply was "Oh that's Verlyn. He is pounding his head against the wall! "In disbelief I asked "isn't he getting hurt?" "No" she said. "He probably does repetitive acts like that to reduce his stress." I said "We better list this act as one we need to reduce and end." We never completely succeeded in that effort but we did succeed in reducing the number of times he inflicted this on himself and others. He never seemed to be injured in any of these bouts and when we sought to stop them he would usually respond with a tired smile.

Naomi was ten years old and served as a mother to Becca. They played often with Naomi combing Becca's hair and dressing her up in various old clothing. Of course Verlyn shared in the activity and together they shared a lot of play time. Verlyn also enjoyed great comfort by trailing Boots around or sitting cross legged with him on the front step of our house while beating on the step with a long stick.

As idyllic as all this seems there was also a "down" side. He did not enjoy leaving his comfort zone to do things that required his attendance at friend's homes or school functions. When confronted by those situations he frequently sat down and refused to move. The whole family tried to coax him into moving. Becca had the best success. Naomi and

Tom tried pushing and if that failed Betty tried a few pleadings which sometimes worked. If all else failed I was the "enforcer." I coaxed and pleaded, pulled and pushed until he surrendered and walked. He showed few signs of anger and never any injury. He would put his smile on his face and often repeated "Verlyn shouldn't act that way" as he trudged along behind others of the family.

Over time the head pounding and sit downs diminished in number" and severity but the efforts took its toll. One day while pulling on Verlyn to get him to move I felt a wave of guilt for me and the members of our disrupted family. I made up my mind "enough" and I began action to arrange a different situation for him outside our home. Like the sale of our farm it was a bitter sweet solution.

We did feel that Verlyn had improved while with our family and indeed he lived successfully the rest of his days in group homes. When we occasionally visited with him he always remembered each of us by our names and recalled important events. He remained special friends with Becca and Boots! He lived long for one with Downs Syndrome and died in his fifties.

These memories were the reason we responded poorly to Wally's challenge to us to join them as foster parents to unaccompanied Vietnamese minors. During the following week Betty and I discussed it but not seriously. After another few days we relented a bit and we agreed to take a look at pictures they had of children that were available. When we requested pictures many came with up to four children in the same family. We decided we just could not split up families. One picture caught our eye. It pictured two small brothers leaning against a telephone pole. We were sold on them. We put in our order and within weeks they arrived at our door accompanied by a social worker. Meanwhile Wally was informed that their boy would not arrive!

Our house was well suited for the increase in family size. During the previous year we had put our house up for sale. With three children at the age when they were in many after school activities we were on the road repeatedly. When a 26 acre field within walking distance of the school became available we bought it and had a large house constructed on the site. The land also had three buildings on it as well for any animals we wanted. With those ideal accommodations we believed we could provide a good living experience for the enlarged family! As we visited with them we discovered the brothers were older than we thought. The youngest boy was nine years old and his name was Hung (pronounced hum). His older brother was fourteen and his name was Minh (pronounced mun}. They were very small physically but very capable survivors. (Wally also soon received two replacements).

We soon discovered that the first and most important problem was to communicate with them. They spoke and understood no English. That would require much help from the entire family. We all learned to pick up a fork or spoon, hold it up and repeat the word over and over again In that way they gradually acquired a limited vocabulary. Another problem surfaced when we discovered that Betty's mother and other members of her family were opposed to our decision to bring the boys into our family. Fortunately that problem would resolve itself with time.

One day while I was harvesting the field which surrounded our house Minh rode with me in our small pickup truck. I knew he would have had no opportunity to drive a vehicle. I explained how the truck operated to drive. The difficulty in communication caused me to wonder how much he understood but I didn't think much about it. Some weeks later we decided to attend the State Fair in the twin cities. We planned to drive there early in the morning and return the following evening. The family was used to that schedule because Tom and Naomi had previously participated in the music competition at the Fair. Minh protested saying that he did not want to accompany the family. We were surprised but Betty felt that his reluctance was from a sick feeling he sometimes had when riding in a vehicle. We were a little concerned about his staying home by himself but I felt that someone who had survived his previous life could certainly survive a day by himself.

After attending the fair we returned home. As we drove in the tree lined approach to our house I saw the truck parked in its usual place near the garage but as we parked near the truck it was apparent that the cab was badly damaged! When we entered the house we discovered a note written by Minh. The note informed us that he had driven the truck and had damaged it. He then informed us that he was leaving our house and family and pleaded with us to take care of Hung! Soon we learned the entire story. When we left he had invited another Vietnamese boy to join him. When it was time for his guest to return home Minh offered to drive him to his home in the truck. He also brought our cat with them in the cab of the truck. He then drove down the hill through the field in reverse across the ditch and onto the road. He then drove the boy home, returned and a short distance from our house the cat jumped on him. He swerved the truck and it rolled on its side in the middle of the road. Coincidentally our Sheriff friend was close behind him. He helped get the truck on its wheels and waited for our return.

The damage to the truck was a minor concern. The major problem was where to find Minh. Betty guessed where he was so she called a Vietnamese family that had attended our church. Their oldest girl answered the phone. "Yes" she said "he was there but he was very upset and she urged "would we please be kind to him?" We were very relieved he was found and we retrieved him. We let him know that it was a bad thing to do but it was not a serious problem that couldn't be dealt with. All that was delivered partly by sign language and partly by words but mostly by quiet emotion. Privately we were more relieved than he was and neither of us wanted to pursue it further. It was soon forgotten as a "small pothole" on an otherwise smooth road.

Minh and Hung began school at their skill levels. Then they advanced two grade levels each year until they graduated from High School. They also attended English classes until they could satisfactorily overcome the language problem. Upon graduation from High School they both entered the community college at the appropriate time. We tried to teach them both about Jesus while we were still attending the Bethlehem Lutheran Church and when they requested to be baptized Pastor Jim complied and they became Christians. Jesus in the power of the Holy Spirit had chosen them out of millions of Vietnamese people to join our family and his.

The number of children living in our home had grown from three to five. Then before we realized it the number returned to three. As I lay in bed one morning in a semi state of sleep consciousness I felt someone sit next to me on the bed. It was Tom. I awakened because it was strange for Tom to enter our bedroom. He looked down at me and said "Dad, I want to get married!" "What" I thought "you are only seventeen." I was not aware he had ever dated a girl or even thought of girls in a romantic way. He had only been interested in fishing, hunting and cars to my knowledge. After the initial shock Betty and I visited with him and we discovered that the object of his affection was a classmate named Angie. He said she also wanted to be married. When our first reaction calmed down we resolved to call Angie's parents and after considerable discussion both families agreed that perhaps it was a good idea! Angie was a remarkable girl and Tom was capable of taking a mature attitude in what would probably be a difficult world of work. Besides they were in love with each other. They married, finished their senior year of school, and advanced to the Community College. Naomi had already attended a year at the University of North Dakota when she arrived with a similar request. She wanted to marry a local boy named Mark Cole. By this time Betty and I were almost professional at young marriages. They were married, continued their education at the Community College and produced a girl baby named Jessica. By then Tom and Angie had also produced a boy baby named Joshua. Our family at home was back to three but our real family was now nine. Praise the Lord.

Our family living at home soon was reduced again. This time it was Minh who decided to leave. Shortly after Minh and Hung arrived in our family we had learned much of their experiences before leaving Viet Nam. Of course we realized that the United States involvement in Viet Nam had ended with the withdrawal of U. S. troops. The government of Viet Nam was replaced by a North Vietnamese communist government. The communist government then conscripted most young men into the army. One of those affected by that proclamation was Hung and Minh's older brother. Rather than serve he chose to flee. The government then decided that his two younger brothers (eight year old Hung and twelve year old Minh) would have to replace him in the communist army. Their parents responded by secretly obtaining passage for them on a boat that was sailing out of the country with an overloaded number of people on board. The parents of Minh and Hung did not even inform the boys they were to leave until the time the boat was nearly ready to sail. Minh was charged by their parents to take care of his younger brother.

When the boat was loaded they were ordered to stay below deck with little food or water. The trip would last for six days and five nights before it docked at an island in Indonesia named Galang. While on the voyage a woman seated beside Hung died. At Galang several nations from around the world had representatives to divide the young refugees for resettlement in each of their various nations. Minh and Hung were selected by representatives of the United States to come to America but they had to wait until families in America agreed to receive them. We were one of those families. Both boys were small in stature when they arrived. Hung eventually grew to about five feet ten in height but Minh did not grow much beyond five feet in height. Minh was very muscular and was quite successful in high school wrestling.

Minh was doing well in his second year at the community college but interrupted his final quarter as a student to join the regular United States Army. After his experience escaping the Communist army I was especially surprised that he would join the U.S Army but we were proud of him. His choice became his career. He joined the most responsible and dangerous part of the army called "special forces." The American nation received a valuable return on their investment in Minh. When I visit with him on the telephone he occasionally tells me that he reads his Bible each day. Praise the Lord!

A RECENT PHOTO Minh is pictured in his dress uniform and will be retired in 2011 as a warrant officer. Hung is pictured beside him. He continues to work as a chef in the Mountain View Hospital in Mesa Arizona. He is also developing a catering service which is growing and will soon require his full time. Two friends raised by the Wallace Nesses in Fergus Falls are pictured beside them. Both are smaller in stature than Minh and Hung but very large in ability. The oldest named Hau earned a Masters Degree in Electrical Engineering but continues to work outside his field in private business. He has organized a foundation which created and maintains three orphan homes in Viet Nam. His brother Chau pictured beside him served in the U.S. Peace

Corps. Both boys are ardent Roman Catholic Christians and live with their wives and children in North Carolina. Four brothers and sisters have joined them there. They now include two medical doctors, a dentist, and a nurse.

Becca and Hung were our remaining family. They enjoyed each other and did a lot of things together. Hung's main interest was anything related to food preparation. He was Betty's gift from God. He prepared meals when she didn't and we all learned to enjoy egg rolls and other oriental food which he seemed to prepare better than others. As time passed he acquired interests in anything that interested others including an interest in God. His interests were evidenced by a kind of "bubbly" excitement and an approving giggle.

Becca was our scholar. As a teacher I admired the fact that she had the finest study habits and discipline imaginable which led to a straight "A" average and the roll of valedictorian in her High School class. Becca and Hung accompanied Betty and I through the time of learning and participating in the Holy Spirit "wave" that continued to sweep many in the nation into the nineties. Somewhere along the way she was filled with the Holy Spirit and she lived her faith. Many girls from high school and college seemed to group around her as their leader. She was very attractive so she also had boys grouped around her. One of the boys was a nice young man who dated her during much of her high school and college days. She liked him but was concerned by the fact that he was unsaved and did not seem very interested in things spiritual.

Our family attended Mt. Carmel Bible Camp near Alexandria, Minnesota frequently during the beautiful days of summer. Occasionally we also drove to a Bible camp located at Strawberry Lake North of Detroit Lakes, It was a Pentecostal type of Bible camp and Becca especially enjoyed young people that camped there. One weekend she decided to drive to the camp and while there she met a young man named Rob Ketterling. They had a good time together and a short time later she attended the camp again. During an evening session where a number of youth were gathered a woman had a prophesy. She prophesied that there was a young girl present there who had been dating a boy over a period of time but that God had something else in mind for her. Becca knew immediately that the prophesy was meant for her so she went to the telephone and broke up with her boyfriend. Rob had been at the lake and on his way back to his twin cities home he was very depressed. He had come to the conclusion that Becca was the girl he sought for a wife but that was not possible now because she had not broken with her boyfriend. Upon arrival home Rob received a call in which Becca informed him that she had in fact broken with her boyfriend.

Over the next several months that relationship flourished and Rob asked her to marry him. She was reluctant to answer him but she confided to her Mom that she would decide by Christmas. With that slender hope Rob prepared for Christmas by inviting Becca to share her Christmas with his family. He then bought an engagement ring put it on a long stemmed rose and placed it in a typical dress box. Rob's mother Isabel entered into the scheme with gusto by asking Becca her dress sizes. Meanwhile Becca had made up her mind to accept his proposal! She also prepared for Christmas with a card in which she had written that any girl would be happy to marry him etc., but she hoped she would be the one. (Later Betty asked him what he would have done if she had said "no". He replied that he would have thrown up) after that the only hurdle preventing their marriage was me! I had hoped that she would finish her education before marriage as she was very young. Of course I was outnumbered (Becca,

Mom, his folks and God were tough to overcome). Rob and Becca agreed. Without a church building the Lutheran Brethren Church was rented and Lord Jesus Fellowship Pastor Dan Mueller presided at the marriage ceremony.

Rob became a youth Pastor in a St. Cloud, Minnesota Assembly of God Church and two years later Becca graduated with a B.A. Degree from St. Cloud State University. Only Hung remained at home and he soon graduated from the Community college with a two year degree. He decided not to pursue a four year degree and turned to his obsession of food preparation by receiving a certificate as a Chef from the Culinary Institute at Scottsdale, Arizona. Betty and I had an empty nest!

Chapter 12

LORD JESUS FELLOWSHIP RECEIVES A HOME

L ord Jesus Fellowship was providing an alternative church to a community which was mostly protestant Lutheran. It was not the only alternative. Another charismatic church had begun primarily as a youth group and had grown quickly. It became the Community Bible Church and soon built a large church building. Their numbers grew but the Lord Jesus Fellowship remained with about eight "core families" and a Sunday church attendance of approximately 100 persons. It seemed that a church building was a future necessity. Efforts at raising money for a church building reached about a 70,000 dollar figure and remained at that level. A building committee contacted church building companies but the estimates were beyond our abilities at about 500,000 dollars. Much prayer was not immediately answered.

My personal career as an instructor at the community College was also nearing an end. In the fall of the year 1991 I was eligible for retirement. I had completed ten years of teaching in High School and 24 years in College. Not only would that mean a major career change but also a major change in where we would continue to live. When Betty and I married I had wanted to work in a warm climate. We had agreed to live in a cold climate as long as I worked in my career because both of our families remained in North Dakota and Minnesota. We also agreed that when I had a career change we would move south. Where that would be we did not know but we visited Florida, Texas, California, and Arizona seeking an answer to that question over years of prayerful inquiries.

The answer continued to be unclear at retirement but we made several decisions of an immediate nature. The first was to list our home we had constructed on the 26 acres of land at Fergus Falls. It sold and we moved into an apartment in Fergus Falls. We would have moved into a house on our 160 acre farm located four miles southwest of Fergus Falls which we had purchased two years previously but Tom, Angie and family needed a house more desperately. They had returned from California where Angie had been teaching and they wanted to remain in the Fergus Falls area. Angie was an elementary school teacher but there were few school openings as a result they moved into the farm house and we agreed to farm together in a "hog operation". After one year it became obvious it was not profitable so I closed it down. I continued to farm the land while Tom took jobs in construction. In the midst of our "hog farming" year Betty and I discovered a house on a desirable lake near Battle Lake seventeen miles east of Fergus Falls. We bought it with my promise to Betty that we would enlarge the house with the immediate addition of a sun room and other remodeling. Much of the finishing work I undertook during my "free time."

With all the "free time" I also drew up a plan for a church that I thought might meet our needs. I then visited the manager of a local lumber yard that I knew to be a Christian and together we developed an estimate of about 150,000 dollars. Much more reasonable then other estimates. Then submitted the plan to the church group and they said "go ahead" with me continuing on as the general contractor. No Problem! I had all that retirement "free time".

Pastor Hanson, a Luther Seminary trained Lutheran replaced Pastor Dan as the building process began. The people of the congregation continued to worship and praise the Lord while contributing both time and money. They were wonderful! A carpenter crew from Ashby did most of the framing and some of the finishing. Local businesses were employed to provide plumbing, heating, brick work etc. Of course the land had been provided by Bob and Ruby Torkelson. In that way we built our own beautiful church for a total of 160,000 dollars which we completely paid off in three years.

Chapter 13

TRIALS AND TRIBULATIONS

Blessed is the man who perseveres under trial,
Because when he has stood the test,
He will receive the crown of life that God
promised to those who love him.
James 1:12

With the church nearing completion Betty and I journeyed to Arizona where we discovered a reasonably priced double wide mobile home in a lovely park in Mesa. We bought it and began a yearly schedule in which we lived at the lake in Minnesota during the summer months and our home in Mesa during the winter months. In the days of Bethlehem Church attendance I read a booklet on prayer. It suggested that a person should spend an hour a day in prayer. How impossible I thought. With the baptism of the Spirit and the needs of an elder my time in prayer began to expand dramatically. I often began to pray at 5 a.m. as I became aware of so many needs of family, friends, government, church, and private projects that an hour did not provide sufficient time for intercession and praise. The Holy Spirit continued to manifest his gifts in the church and the prayer life of many combined to create a splendid atmosphere in the new church building.

A personal trial began about three years after the construction of the church building was complete. I visited Dr. Bjork's office for my annual physical. He suggested that it was time to take a "stress" test to determine my heart health. I flunked the test! Dr. Bjork then sent me to a cardiologist in Fargo who decided to place a diagnostic dye in my blood stream to check for blockages. Before the test ended I had a "stent" placed in one of my arteries. Later when he discussed the procedure with me he said in an off handed way "oh, by the way did you know that you have had two heart attacks?" Actually I did remember both of them. I just did not know what they were at the time. I simply felt an ache in the area of my breast bone which lasted for about a week each time. I also remember a tiredness which lasted for months afterward.

As we discussed the heart problem I asked the cardiologist if it was possible that I may have an aneurysm because I experienced pain while bending to weed the garden. He replied that an ultra sound test would be a good way to determine that. When he met with me after the test he told me that the good news was that I did not have an aneurysm but the bad news was that I had a growth on my right kidney! Later an Urologist concluded that it could be cancer but that I should have a biopsy. Instead I returned to my regular Dr. Bjork and asked him to send me to the Rochester Mayo clinic. He said "O K" but if it was him he would remain at the Fergus Falls clinic and see Dr. Fraley. He was very intense in his advice so I took my X-rays to Dr. Fraley. When the doctor entered the examining room he put the X-rays on the screen, briefly looked at it and turning to me he said" You have cancer. Go make an appointment for surgery, we have to get it out of there." "But" I said "the urologist said I should have a biopsy" He replied "if that doctor had done that it would have spread." Then I said "Have you ever done that surgery before?" He ignored me as he left the room. I later learned from others that he was near retirement and had been a well-known doctor at the University of Minnesota Hospital who had taught most of the doctors in the upper mid-west how to do that surgery! How about that for God answering our prayers even before we ask. The surgery was a success 15 years ago at this writing. Praise the Lord.

Another trial involved the Lord Jesus Fellowship. Pastor Hanson moved to the University of Iowa to work with foreign students. His replacement was a man from the local area not as well trained as Pastor Hanson but quite popular. Unknown to me and many in the church was his addiction to alcohol. That addiction was not evident at the time he was hired. The first years of his ministry went well with a renewed interest in the gifts of the spirit. Then quietly at first stories began to be rumored about his uncontrolled drinking. Some action was necessary but a disaster intervened!

Early in October of 2001 Art and Dorothy Mueller stopped at the Fergus Falls Wal-Mart store. Art was driving as they left the parking lot. As he prepared to enter Highway. 210 a vehicle with a camper started to pull off the road. A car traveling fast behind the camper and shielded from Art's view collided with Art's car as he turned onto the road. It hit him on the driver's door and killed Art instantly. Dorothy who was beside him on the passenger seat was also seriously injured and bruised but survived. A very sad day! The church would suffer from the loss of his guiding presence.

The funeral was held at the Lutheran Brethren Bethel Church to accommodate a very large crowd. Many of the people were those who had been touched by his ministry. Included were two brothers who had driven in from Montana to express their thankfulness for his impact on their lives. Bob played the accordion and for the first time in many of the mourner's memory a funeral crowd applauded after his rendition. Many persons spoke lovingly of their memories of Art and the mood was that of celebration which indeed it was. The day of the funeral Pastor Arden entered counseling for alcohol addiction. It was the last day of his ministry at the Fellowship. Months later I resigned the position of elder. I was in Arizona for too long periods of time to be effective. When I was in Minnesota there were various demands on my time also. I farmed, I taught a weekly bible study in rural Elbow Lake, and drove from the Lake for meetings. When I resigned the congregation was doing fine. There was good leadership from within and they filled the vacancy positions in the deacons and elder boards. They in turn persuaded Pastor Dan to return for a third time. As a former elder I have not missed a day of prayer for the Fellowship that I remember to the present. The Holy Spirit never resigned or left. The present numbers are between two and three hundred parishioners. Praise the Lord. Pastor Dan has been the head elder and pastor since 2003 and recently his son Jeremy has helped with a ministry to the youth. (Art's grandson}

Six months of each year after 1993 we have lived in Mesa Arizona. Betty and I attended a small bible group at a park where we lived termed Palmas del Sol. The bible group was led by Herb Atwood a former leader in the Navigators, and Owen Burke, a retired Nazarene pastor. Three or four others rounded out the group. After I regained some strength from my bout with cancer I became the teacher of the group which gradually increased in numbers until the numbers averaged between fifteen and thirty five depending on the month. I realized I was back doing what I was gifted to do. To teach. The group was mostly in their sixties, seventies, or eighties. Precious saints of the Lord! Herb led one man to the Lord who was in his eighties! A rare happening. Previously he had been a "rounder" but when he came to the Lord he took on a sweet personality who was a pleasure to teach. Much of our time during summer months Betty and I took the opportunity to attend the Good shepherd Lutheran Brethren

Church where our son and family attended. It was a blessing to watch them all grow.

One trial remains to explain. It is a post script from the days when we attended the Bethlehem Lutheran Church. Pastor Jim seemed to Bob and me to be placing pressure on us over the adult class content concerning the Holy Spirit. We felt the Holy Spirit was initiating a revival in the church through the adult class. Pastor Jim appeared to be a solid man in his beliefs and we had no quarrel with him personally. He often praised his wife Lois and other family members from the pulpit. Some considerable time after we left the Church we were surprised to hear that he and his wife had separated. Later we heard that they had divorced and their children reportedly supported Pastor Jim but rejected their mother Lois.

Bob and Ruby were our close friends and they also settled in Arizona near us and stayed the entire winter. One day Bob surprised us with the information that Lois was a nurse and was employed in Phoenix. He had visited with her and learned that her family had rejected her except for her youngest son Paul who lived mostly in San Francisco, California. Later he heard the rumor that he was gay and Lois was trying to help and watch over him.

Over the years Betty and I and Bob and Ruby tried to invite her with us for various events and celebrations to help her feel less rejected. One day we stopped by her condo in Phoenix, We visited with her and learned she was going to move to a friend's house to live. There she believed she would be happier then where she currently lived. The day before she was to move Bob and Ruby stopped by to visit on their annual trip back to Minnesota. While they visited she repeated how happy she would be because of her proposed move. She was packed and boxes were piled around ready to move.

The next morning her son Paul called us and shocked us with the news that she had died over night. We visited with Bob and Ruby over the phone and we agreed that we would attend the funeral when we learned of the time and place. The funeral was to be held at a large Lutheran church in Phoenix. The traffic was heavy on our way to the funeral and we arrived late. We found it very difficult to find the entrance to the church or even cars in the parking lot. Finally we found an entrance and a woman approached us saying we were late but that we could join the hand full of people who were assembled there. After the remaining ceremony we again visited with the lady who had told us that we were late. As we visited we asked her how she had died so suddenly. She replied "Oh, didn't' you know? She took her own life! A letter she had written was read at the beginning of the funeral in which she explained her action". We returned to our car bewildered. It was like the whole family had exploded. Some may suggest that it was because Pastor Jim had blocked the Holy Spirit in producing a revival at the Bethlehem church, I don't believe that and neither do I hold any anger of any type. It happened. I know little and I don't want to know more. I think the Holy Spirit grieved with us.

Chapter 14

CHANGES! AN EPILOGUE

I was born into a European church. I did not have to live in Europe to be born into a European church. The Norwegian Lutheran Church came with immigrants from Norway trying to escape the grinding poverty which was characteristic of those in Norway. Other peoples from around the nation belonged to European churches as well. They were Germans, Swedish people, French and many others. They brought their language, folkways, and their mores when they immigrated and they were comfortable in duplicating their beliefs wherever they settled. God the Father was hallowed, Jesus was the savior of those who believed, and the Holy Spirit was mentioned as God but not well identified. The Holy Spirit had acted in the formation of the European church in Europe so it was not wrong. It did need change to the unique needs of America.

One obvious need was to accommodate Romans 10: 17 *"Faith comes by hearing and hearing by the word of God."* Young people or persons who did not understand the language used by the church remained "faithless!" English in schools, the army, business and legal work needed to also be adopted by the various churches. Some parishioners fought against change such as my Grandfather Halvor but they too eventually changed. In addition the various churches changed their names to emphasize that people of all languages were welcome. The Norwegian Lutheran Church was renamed the Evangelical Lutheran Church. Other churches with national identity in their title made similar changes. The Latin used by the Catholic Church trailed many others in language change but when the tide of the Holy Spirit rushed in they were among the leaders.

The mid twentieth century pushed many churches into changes unimagined by earlier moves of the Holy Spirit. The earthquake of the early twentieth century was World War I and then World War II. Many boys experienced battle field conversions while others were exposed to strong life style changes. These experiences led to a tidal wave of change throughout society. The strength of the wave led some to call it a tsunami. One of the first and most important portions of the wave made its appearance in the 1950s and 1960s. It was a dramatic rise of gospel and worship music. It put emotion and words to a personal relationship with God. Nearly every church whether conservative or liberal adopted and maintained at least a portion of the new music for worship if only among the youth.

Technology advances such as radio, TV, low priced books, movies, and voice magnification enabled the gospel to spread to the multitudes of people. Billy Graham and other evangelists used the new methods to issue a call to the masses. The wave carried by mass media even moved the gospel back to the homeland of the American immigrants as well as darkest Africa and Asia. If the wave of the Holy Spirit accompanied by advances in technology could be compared to a wave of water the wave of water would be expected to diminish, become shallow and stall out. The wave of the Holy Spirit also appeared to diminish. A water wave could be expected to remain in steams and puddles.

The Holy Spirit as well seemed to diminish and flow into streams and puddles.

Jesus prophesied that action with the Parable of the Sower. A farmer scattered seed in which some was eaten by birds, other seed fell on shallow soil and was burned by the sun, other seed fell on ground where thorns sprang up and choked the plant, but some seed fell on good ground and produced a bountiful crop.

As an artist painting a portrait of the Holy Spirit it would be easy to say the Holy Spirit just gives up on the "high ground." If that thought was accepted the hard working pastors and well-meaning congregations and the work of the Holy Spirit would fail. That the only people saved would be those born in good ground and displaying growth from good ground. I want to portray the Holy Spirit as a person with the tenacity of Jesus who refused to call legions of angels to save him and endured the cross to save those who believe on him. Instead I would paint a Holy Spirit who would combine persistence with the developments and changes of the modern world. And if that doesn't save more people my Holy Spirit would persuade Jesus to return to earth with him on a new and greater wave!

Where would such a wave be found? As a historian I would look to the streams and puddles to see what could be learned from their success. Such a stream may not be in America. China is thought by many to have the largest number of Christians in the world. How can that be possible? It is a repressive police state where Christians are persecuted. Perhaps the answer is that persecution has forced Christians into small house churches where personal faith leads to action which overcomes the forces waiting to pick up the seed. In a small house church leadership otherwise undiscovered may be found. Gifts of the Holy Spirit may be manifested. Fruit of the Spirit displayed. Loving friends with individual needs can present loving prayers to a loving father

God. House churches are not new. They were an important part of the early church. Perhaps even mega churches need house churches to be successful whether in China or anywhere churches of any size are formed. When my Grandfather Halvor homesteaded his farm the parable of the sower would apply to farm methods of the day. Seed indeed was scattered on virgin soil. It grew subject to the quality of the soil and conditions during the season of growth. Some was eaten by birds, some died because of shallow and unfertile soil, while other seed was choked by weeds.

With similar conditions the modern farmer plants in soil which is fertilized and prepared by powerful tractors. The seed is planted to the depth where birds cannot destroy. If lack of moisture prevents a crop the land is irrigated. Herbicide eliminates choking weeds. Even the seed would be of hybrid vitality. Soil maps are created to describe the needs of each acre. All the input costs can be financed by loans guaranteed by crop insurance.

When I retired from teaching at the age of 56 I did not retire from work. I had grown up on a farm, practiced part time farming, and began a farming venture near Fergus Falls which would last for 17 years. At the same time I was undertaking and learning a new career our daughter Becca (for whom God prophesied that he had something better for her in mind} and her husband Rob Ketterling were beginning a church in a suburb of Minneapolis termed Rosemont. The industry of agriculture was undergoing massive changes and so too was the development of churches. Rob agreed with Becca that if she worked for one year she should be able to quit and the church would be self-sufficient. Ten years later the church was sufficient to allow her to quit work. Rob noted the event by filling her office with ten dozen roses!

When Rob Ketterling began the River Valley Church modern methods also played big and increasing rolls. The number of people available was only limited by the efforts made to reach out to them. Mass mailings invited everyone in the area to attend meetings first in rented schools and later in a rented business building. The gospel was the seed! Unlike the simple scattering of seed technical methods made the scattering of seed difficult for anyone to ignore the welcome. Increases in computer methods, the internet, I Pads. Many other technical methods made it possible to target certain persons and areas much like agricultural mapping of individual acres. As the numbers of those attending increased the amount of money also increased. Ten per cent of all income was allocated for missions. 50 per cent of income was allocated for salaries within the River Valley Church. Tithing was encouraged and 20 per cent of all givers became tithers. Large amounts of money made it possible to employ pastors, counselors, and other support persons. It also allowed additional growth.

One method of growth chosen was to grow by repeating the method used to build the River Valley Church and share various staff by organizing new groups as a campus. An important example of sharing is that the sermon delivered in the mother church was also presented by H D television on a large screen to each of the other campuses. The use of campuses in conjunction with a mother church allowed expansion into a target area without providing the large sums of money necessary to build a mega church building capable of containing the increased numbers. Pastors and support people were then employed for the work of local organization and ministry, (watering, bird hunting and weed picking). In the year 2010 the River Valley Church along with its three campus churches was listed number 67th in the nation of the "fastest growing" churches in the nation. Sunday church attendance averaged between three and four thousand. Plans are being made for more campuses. The River Valley Church is one of a number of Holy Spirit streams designed to improve the numbers of persons and fields that are "ripe onto the harvest." Farmers stand ready to harvest their fields with powerful combines. So too is the church ready to bring in the harvest. Perhaps other ways and means will also contribute to a great new wave of the Holy Spirit but those like the River Valley Church will contribute mightily to the stream of outreach. I believe house churches will continue in the puddles and also in the rivers where the church of Jesus Christ genuinely flourishes

With that the last brush stroke is placed. Each story, thought, and event has formed an image of God in the Holy Spirit who interacts with his creation in mercy, grace, and love. Praise the Lord!

Now every good portrait needs a frame. Come with me in the Spirit as we join the hundreds of people in the old Minneapolis auditorium, a place I know where God is only a "WHOOSH" away! Despite the hundreds of people involved there is a profound silence. Then off in the distance a sound like a swarm of bees gathers intensity. It is the people singing in tongues. The sound grows louder until the auditorium resounds with the glorious sound. Gradually the sound retreats into the profound silence.

Next a single sweet voice breaks the silence with the words:

JESUS JESUS JESUS
MASTER, SAVIOR, JESUS
LIKE THE FRAGRANCE AFTER THE RAIN
MASTER, SAVIOR, JESUS
LET ALL HEAVEN AND EARTH PROCLAIM
KINGS AND KINGDOMS WILL ALL PASS AWAY
BUT THERE IS SOMETHING ABOUT THAT NAME

Again the silence returns except for the people as they raise their hands in unison and loudly sing:

I EXALT YOU

I EXALT YOU

I EXALT YOU OOH LORD

I EXALT YOU

I EXALT YOU

I EXALT YOU OOH LORD

With that the frame is formed and the portrait complete!

9 781612 158297